COMMONSENSE FLY FISHING

COMMONSENSE FLY FISHING

Ray Ovington

Stackpole Books

Published by
STACKPOLE BOOKS
Cameron and Kelker Streets
P.O. Box 1831
Harrisburg, PA 17105

Printed in the U.S.A.

Library of Congress Cataloging in Publication Data

Ovington, Ray.
    Commonsense fly fishing.

    Includes index.
    1. Fly fishing. I. Title.
SH456.0884   1983   799.1´2   82-17029
ISBN 0-8117-2167-1 (pbk.)

Contents

Introduction

When I first discussed the writing of this book with my editors at Stackpole, a publisher that has presented several of my books in the past, David Detweiler handed me a trade-magazine article devoted to the retail sales of fishing tackle. The gist of the article was that fly-fishing equipment is currently benefitting from an upsurge in popularity such as it has never before experienced. Spinning, levelling off now after the boom of its early years, has introduced an entire generation to fishing . . . and now many members of that generation are branching out into fly fishing. The younger generation too is interested—and shows promise of developing into a clan of anglers with a concern for conservation greater and more intense than that of the generation preceding.

Fly fishing and conservation-mindedness are nearly synonymous. Organizations such as TROUT UNLIMITED and THE FEDERATION OF FLY FISHERS are not the machinations of a few old codgers. They have big nationwide memberships and are actively approaching the steps of Capitol Hill. . . .

Why fly fishing? Because it is the highest form of sport fishing yet developed. It gives the fish the most sporting chance to size up the offering, and the gear needed to float a fly properly is much lighter and more fragile and therefore more sporting. The moments of striking, playing, and landing are thrilling. The act of delivering the fly (particularly one you've tied yourself) is a pleasure the average bait fisherman never experiences. The hit is felt right through to the tips of your toes. And of course the battle of playing and landing, especially with a big fish, can be exciting beyond belief.

There's something magical about fly fishing. There have been more books written about this unusual sport than about any other, and the literature is increasing. While I was living in California it was my distinct pleasure to know Mark Kerridge, who, before passing on to dry-fly heaven, gave his 10,000-book collection of angling books to the University of California at Fullerton. . . .

One gets the impression that fishing—fly fishing especially— is an important part of our culture and development as a people.

During the last twenty years, however, we as a people have gone through dramatic changes. And these changes have been reflected in a wide range of cultural activity. Many outmoded values and dogmas have gone by the boards. . . .

In the realm of fly fishing though, I chance the opinion that a great amount of dogma still persists. Even some of the most recent books adhere to many of the earliest tenets of the sport, set down over a hundred years ago.

The book you have in your hands is an attempt to bring some common sense to fly fishing, taking advantage of the traditions of the past not as dogma, but as forms to be improved upon by personal experimentation—or even rejected—when circumstances warrant. The intelligent angler of today can assimilate all the good of the past and use it as a springboard for further development in technique, tying, tackle development, and presentation.

This author has grown up fly fishing. My father was of the old school and taught me how to cast before I could work in fractions. I had the opportunity to meet and see George La Branche cast his flies on the Neversink. I watched Dad fish the Millionaire's Pool for salmon on the Restigouche. He was a good friend of Albert Hendrickson, for whom the Hendrickson fly is named. I personally fished with Edward Hewitt on his private water on the Neversink in the New York Catskills. John Alden Knight and I helped a number of tackle companies develop rod and line tapers. Jim Deren of the Angler's Roost in New York City got me started writing about fishing, and Charles DeFeo, Harry and Elsie Darbe, and a host of others helped me learn to tie a decent fly.

These companions all perpetrated the classic fly-fishing dogma, which of course greatly affected me . . . but I've also been greatly affected along the way by many a non-famous expert—a guide, or a fisherman I just happen to meet on the stream who brings me down to size with his ability to catch fish when I can't.

Yes, there's a lot to learn about fly fishing, and not all of it is in the books.

The trout is a simple creation. He goes about his life naturally, attuned to his environment and what it can offer him. The stream is no secret to him. To us however, it is a mystery. Many who have gone before me have been partially successful in penetrating the mystery, and as a result, like many prophets who have had revelations, have developed their own dogma and followers.

I strive for no such thing. I only want to share what little I have learned, and to emphasize that often the commonsense approach is inhibited by tradition. I want you to carry with you the traditions and developments of the past, and use them when you see fit, but more importantly to develop your own techniques and theories as you "do your own thing."

Experiment! There's nothing more ridiculous than the over-educated angler wading forth with the memorized rules of a hundred fishing texts buzzing in his brain, determined to follow those rules regardless of environment, stream situation, and fish behavior. Don't fall into the trap of letting the fishing writers do your thinking for you. They know more than you do, yes. But in any given situation you have the power on your own to figure out a strategy that will succeed . . . if only you're not afraid to work.

Read the books—this one included—for entertainment and for tips. But don't ever think there's a system, whether for casting or nymphing or drifting or any other facet of fly-fishing, that cannot be vastly improved upon by the application of plain old-fashioned common sense.

Choosing and Learning
How to Use Your Tackle

It isn't the rod that makes the caster. It's training the wrist and forearm to harness the power of the rod by pressuring the sections: the lower, the middle, and the tip.

Let me show you what I mean.

Take any rod, one with a soft-action, medium, or stiff tip. (To perform this experiment a medium-action is best since it is not designed to do anything other than distribute the pressures more or less evenly.)

Before you put the line on it, flex the rod in the usual way. Next flex the rod concentrating on putting pressure on the area just above your hand, allowing the rest of the rod to go its own way. Now concentrate on the last two feet of the tip and flex the rod so only this much of it is activated. Now do the same with the mid-section. You've had three different rods in your hand at once!

Now. Cast a normal forty-foot cast as you would usually do. Fine. Okay now make another cast, only this time concentrate on bending the rod area just above your hand, allowing the rest of the rod to follow through in the action. You have found power you didn't know you had, merely by pressuring the lower end of the rod. Cast again, only this time work just the very tip of the rod, falsecasting, allowing the middle and lower sections to follow through. See the difference? By working just the very tip of the rod you have heightened your accuracy and can direct the fly much better.

The big trick is to start your cast from the power position, that is, working the lower section to activate the cast. The middle section is felt as the swing part of the cast, and the tip section is used for direction and control.

You can adjust practically any rod to your needs—even a stiff-tipped rod—by this method of power accent. A stiff-tipped rod can be made to perform like a soft-tipped rod. A rod with not much bottom strength can be strengthened by pressuring the lower section and allowing the rest of the rod to follow through and balance out.

So what's all this fuss about rod tapers and rod design that has captivated the professional and amateur rod makers all these years? Well, they want to design a rod that will perform at least one function well. They design a stiff tip—but it's too stiff for light leaders and small flies. Until they learn to zone it out, the rod demands too much effort. So next they design a rod with a stiff middle and a softer tip—and it doesn't direct the flies as it should unless they zone it. They come up with a stiff-lower-section rod and it's a dog to cast and line control is lost because only the middle and upper sections are working properly—again, until it's zoned.

While it's fun to design rods and keep on experimenting, just where is it all leading to?

Add the variance among individual casters and you have a collection of elements that can never be systematized. One person is highly energetic and casts as if he were trying to break down a barn door. Another person will handle the rod lightly, easily, softly. How in heaven's name can you find a rod that will accommodate them?

It is my belief that the balance in tackle starts with the angler himself. As you showed yourself in the experiment of pressuring the three rod sections, the personality of the angler in great measure dictates the way he will cast. It is all well and good to tell him he should do this and that, but in the final analysis, after he has been casting for a while he will develop his own pace, speed, and timing and begin to allow the three rod sections to function for him.

When I'm teaching I demonstrate the ease of casting by grasping the rod with just my thumb and forefinger and making a gentle cast—and the 40-foot cast lays out perfectly.

Remember this important point: It's not the *force* with which you move your casting hand that determines the length and accuracy of your cast—it's the *smoothness* and *speed*. Even for power casts, the rod responds to style. Tensed muscles help the weight-lifter, not the fisherman.

So relax your grip. Work your rod from the wrist for the short casts. Then later begin to use your forearm, your upper arm, and for the long power casts (when necessary) even your upper body.

The medium-action rod will work for anyone who can learn to manipulate the three rod zones properly. There are a lot of rod makers, and what they call medium action can vary quite a bit. Within this variation however, it is quite true that for normal distance casting, the angler who has been taught properly to know his rod and to work the power zones will be able to deliver his flies far enough, accurately enough, and smoothly enough so that he won't tire.

If that same angler were to try a stiffer action rod he would have to make adjustments in his casting. This would take some time, and perhaps it would not be worth the changeover, since he would be casting unnaturally.

When I teach classes in fly fishing I have to cast with many different rod actions. When working with a pupil I first cast his rod for him to show him how the line should look in the air. Once I get the feel of his rod I can then start him out with a simple fore-and-aft waving action of the rod for the short line cast. When he gets the feel of this he can begin gradually to lengthen his cast. When he has about forty feet of line in the air, I suggest he begin to learn the zones of power THAT ARE BUILT INTO THAT PARTICULAR ROD. Using his casting personality it is then possible to balance him with his rod, and to show him how to start using the rod more effectively.

When a pupil has learned to cast a forty-foot line smoothly I can then offer him several rods and let him cast with each one. After a few lessons the pupil will begin to select the rod he likes because it fits his personal energy drive. Some people go at casting as if they were trying to hit a home run. Others are gentle. It is largely a matter of matchmaking.

But the point is that I teach the pupil to cast well first, and *then* get him or her to choose a rod. Once you've understood and mastered the three zones of power I've been referring to, you're ready to go about picking a rod. But until you've understood and mastered the rod in general, there's no use trying to figure out which particular type is best for you.

And another thing: Don't be afraid to experiment on your own! After you've mastered the solid basics of the fly cast, go ahead and try some subtle variations. Snap your wrist down a little sooner on the forecast and see what your line does. Stop your forecast short and see what happens to your line. Cast sidearm a little. Bring your forearm down in an outside-in curve on the forecast. Cast like a waving willow. Cast sharply and abruptly. Experiment. Observe closely the effects that these variations have on the action of your line. You'll begin to get a more profound feel for the many different ways you can use your rod and line—and then when you sit in your armchair and start reading complicated descriptions of the push cast and the drop cast and the underhand-lift and open-loop, you might actually understand what's going on.

Another part of the balance of angler and rod involves the choice of line weight, softness, and taper. A double-tapered line that is recommended by the rod manufacturer may be too light for the power caster or the fast caster. He should probably go to the next size larger taper. The slow caster, however, can use a smaller-diameter taper and accomplish his forty-foot cast with ease.

Now add the leader. The fast caster is going to find a ten-foot leader hard to handle unless he slows down a bit. The slow caster will find the short leader inadequate for his needs. The leader will slap down too hard for him.

Some of the numerous charts available in the fly-fishing literature give a good *general* idea of which lines, and leaders, match up with which kinds of rods. But beware. A whole collection of variables—your own personal casting style, whether your rod's bamboo or fiberglass or graphite, the size of fly you're going to be using, wind conditions, and a host of other factors—make it impossible to mechanize the process of matching rod to line to leader.

Use common sense. Get out on the stream and experiment and pay close attention to the results. No amount of printed charts and tables can substitute for experience on the water.

Most beginner anglers want to cast a country mile. They want a rod and line combination that will allow them to sail out a sixty-footer. They want to be tournament experts the first time out. They labor under the delusion that fly-casting demands great distance. But although the long cast looks good and feels good, the fly on the end is what's important, and if that fly is not under control at all times, the fisherman will be just casting, not catching.

The desire to reach across the whole stream to that pocket over there by that rock is best fulfilled by wading to a different position. Unless all you want to do is perform, leave the power-casting alone. Those long casts and messy pickups can put a lot of fish down. And furthermore, if you do happen to hook onto a big one after one of those monster casts, with all that line out, and all that water (full of potential hiding places and obstructions) between you and the fish, you're going to have a heck of a time playing and landing.

Out west on the big steelhead rivers, or on the Atlantic salmon streams of New Brunswick, longer casts are supposedly professional-looking. But I can tell you that the salmon I have taken and those I have seen taken by the real experts are hooked on short to medium casts, not the performing-arts series.

I recommend using a long rod. But if it's not necessary to make long casts, you say, why a long rod?

The answer is that your rod is not just for casting. It's for lure presentation, control of drift, and hooking and playing. If you want to keep your line off the water to eliminate drag, or properly tie onto and play in a big fish, or lay out a tricky roll cast under difficult stream conditions, the longer rod helps.

The longer rod is also recommended for the short angler, since it keeps more of his line out of the water when held upright.

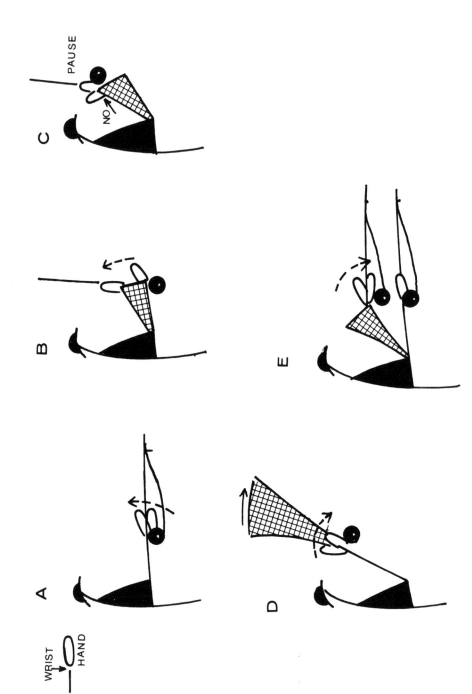

Here we have a go at the conventional fore-and-aft cast, emphasizing the action of the wrist and arm.

The cast schematically depicted here is meant to be on the short side—no longer than 40 feet. It can be accomplished without any line in your hand, if you like. In fact, trying it a few times this way would be good practice.

Note that at every stage the upper arm remains essentially motionless. Only the forearm, with the elbow as its fulcrum, moves up and down.

The beginning of the cast, shown in A, involves the lifting of the wrist to start the rod with a whip on its up-and-back course. This lift of the wrist occurs a split second before the forearm is raised.

B shows the upward flip of the wrist to the vertical, with the forearm raising as a result. In C the forearm is raised as much as necessary for this shortline cast. NOTE: Do not allow your wrist to bend back beyond the vertical. You lose control, power, and touch. In addition your line will probably hit the water behind you.

After a pause—to let the line go out straight behind your head, the forecast is initiated. Again the wrist starts things off (as shown in D). Then the forearm follows through for the dropdown. Note in E that the wrist is still leading (i.e. remains ahead of the forearm), until the very end, when wrist and forearm straighten out and are in line again.

POWER CAST

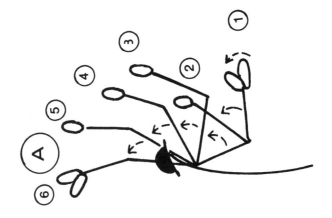

This depicts the power cast.

Essentially this motion is the same as that of the conventional fore-and-aft cast, with an added step for more power.

This step brings into play the upper arm. The wrist action is the same, and as important as ever to ensure an effortless delivery—but now the upper arm moves too.

Starting at (1) the wrist initiates the action and is followed upward first by the forearm (2) and then the upper arm (3). Wrist, forearm, and upper arm move up in concert (4, 5), with the wrist always at the vertical.

At (6) the wrist is allowed a very quick fallback to beyond vertical. Then quickly it is snapped sharply forward to initiate the forecast. This is just a quickie flip, but a strong one. Wrist, forearm, and upper arm come forward as your line comes sailing forward over your head on the forward throw.

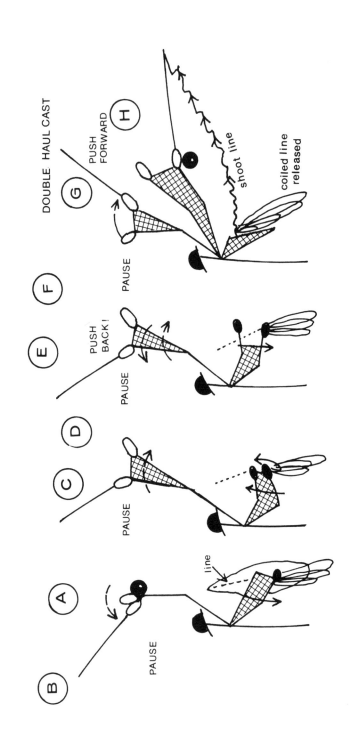

DOUBLE HAUL CAST

The double haul cast is a little difficult to show, but we'll give it a try.

This is a cast that will stand you in good stead when you're facing into a heavy wind, throwing extra-heavy flies, or going for distance. It requires a shooting, or weight-forward, line and a leader well balanced with the weight of the flies you're trying to get out there.

Your right hand is the rod hand, your left hand the line hand. You begin and carry through to the top of the backcast just as you did in the power cast. Then at the top you snap your wrist back past the vertical (again just as in the power cast), and simultaneously draw line in from the rod (B). This builds up more bend and power in the rod.

You pause a split-second, with the line now curling out behind you, and just as it's about to straighten out you push forward with your wrist and just a touch of forearm.

Now comes a second powerful push back (E). This is the second kick of power, meant to send that line back with force, bending the rod back so it will bend equally forward on the forecast and send that line powerfully to its destination.

The push forward (F) turns into a strong one and the line curls forward in a rush powerful enough to carry out through the guides of your rod the extra line you've been holding in your left hand.

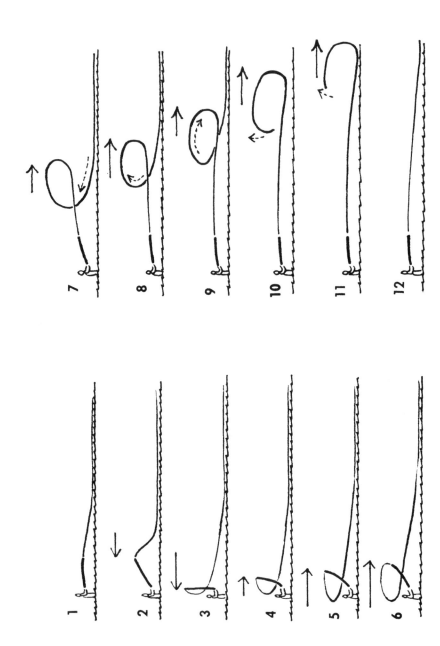

The roll cast: Starting with your line out before you in the in-stream position, bring your rod back up to the vertical in one smooth, quick move. You are not lifting your line off the water. You are sliding it back over the water toward you.

Once your rod and line have reached the ver-tical – as shown in 3 – you are ready to make the forward thrust (4, 5, 6) that will result in the high, wide, loop pattern shown in 7, 8 and 9.

Once you've made the forward thrust the line works on its own, rolling out over itself to come down gently, fully extended, on the water.

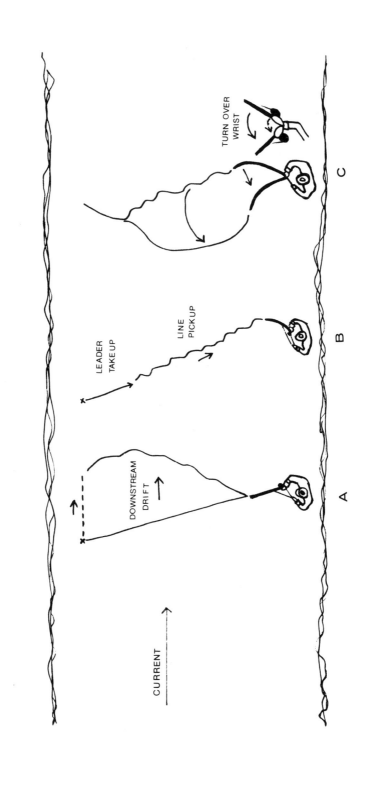

CURRENT

A

DOWNSTREAM
DRIFT

B

LEADER
TAKE UP

LINE
PICKUP

C

TURN OVER
WRIST

The mend cast is simple. As you raise your rod tip, accumulating some slack, push forward on the rod as you would do in the regular forward part of a roll cast, only instead of throwing the line straight out, bend your wrist to the left (assuming you're trying to mend your line to the left – upstream – as shown in the diagram). This points the rod left and swings the rod tip to the left, carrying with it the line-slack that you picked up on the initial pullback. Then, as you bring the rod tip down

– as in the second half of the roll cast – the line will bend into an upstream bow, landing on the water as shown in the diagram.

If you wish to mend your whole line and leader, a broad sweep of the rod is required. If you wish to mend only the end of your line and leader, accent your push with the rod tip only. If you wish to mend the section of line nearest to you, then work the bottom, or butt section of the rod.

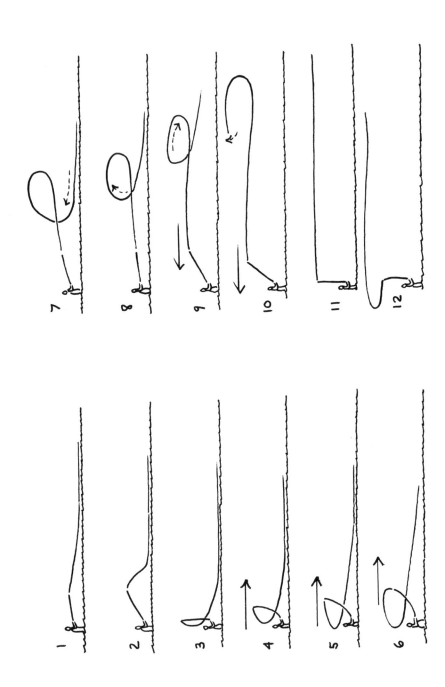

The roll-cast pickup begins the same way as the regular roll cast. Your line is out on the water —either with your rod low (as in 1) or else high (somewhere between 2 and 3).

You draw the rod back and up to the vertical (3), and then initiate the forward thrust (4, 5, 6) that creates the unfurling loop, or roll, that gives the basic roll cast its name. . . .

But this time instead of wanting your line to unfurl out before you onto the water again, you want to get the line into the air over your head in a proper falsecasting, or fore-and-aft-casting position. So long about 9 you start sharply drawing the rod (which in 4 through 8 you've been lowering) back up to the vertical, and the roll-cast loop continues forward, unfurling your line—only now the line's in the air, beginning to form a bow, forming itself into falsecasting, or fore-and-aft-casting position . . . from which of course you can go into whatever next kind of cast you like.

I used to own a six-footer that killed its share of land-locked salmon, Atlantics, smallmouth bass and western trout. But I used that rod when I wanted to live dangerously and push my equipment well beyond its capabilities. As a rule I prefer a longer rod, since it will cast for me with far less effort than I expend with the little six-footer. Also, the big rod is much more versatile. Ever try to rollcast a long line with a little six-foot rod? Ever try to manipulate a nymph well downstream in the current with a short light-action rod?

You can't!

The rollcast pickup, the rollcast mend, throwing upstream loops, and other maneuvers mentioned in this book require a rod that is used more for rollcasting than for conventional fore-and-aft casting. So in considering what rod you should buy, remember to think about rollcasting as a prime necessity.

Most manufacturers offer recommendations with their rods. Read these guides. But if you can test the rods of other anglers you will have a distinct advantage. You'll find that some rods will cast a line to a certain distance well and from there on out require much too much effort and rod strain in order to reach out another ten feet.

I remember a bamboo rod I bought from Wm. Mills in New York some thirty years ago. Arthur Mills asked me to try it for my nymph fishing. It was a beautiful rod and functioned for me with excellence up to about forty or forty-five feet. I could control the cast, keep the line high behind me on the falsecast, and drop those nymphs right on a dime. But to push that rod beyond that point—even with a different line and a longer leader—was almost impossible. The rod was not designed for quick dry-fly fore-and-aft whipping. I could cast dry flies with it of course, but I had to slow down considerably and distance was limited—though it performed with perfection within its limitations.

Today, with the refinements that have come along with fiberglass, plastic, and graphite, we have rods that I'm sorry to say can far outdistance the bamboos of yesteryear . . . but remember, the best and the most fish are caught in close, not way out there.

So my best advice—in general—is: short casts with a medium or long rod . . . after that you're on your own!

Too many of us forget about the leader and its effect on our casting. The relationship between the end of your line and the size and flexibility of your leader must be taken into consideration before a balanced casting performance can be arrived at. A fast-tip rod will not cast a long leader well unless the leader is heavy at the butt end and slowly tapered. If the leader is too fine it will not straighten out quickly enough on a fast falsecast, and so the timing of the cast will have to be slowed greatly, thereby defeating the rod's action. If you insist on a long leader with a fast-action rod and quick snappy casts, take extra care to balance leader with line.

I have experimented with double-tapered leaders and found that by starting out with a small butt section, building to a fifty-percent increase in the center, and then tapering down to say 5X, I can get the leader to straighten out better. You don't hear much about this kind of experimentation, but if you try it you'll discover a lot about what happens up there in the air on your casts.

Spend more time on your leaders. As you develop different types you may have to alter your timing and the distribution of the power in your rod on the cast.

A long leader, for instance, generally requires that you activate the lower part of the rod at the beginning of the cast, then flip your attention to the rod tip at the point of delivery.

Mass distribution and its dramatic changes have definitely affected the tackle industry. Time was when sporting goods were to be found in the local hardware store, or in a specialty shop operated by a fisherman and his wife who specialized in tackle, special flies, and much hand repair and innovation. These still exist, and many flourish, despite the price-cutting chain stores' sporting goods departments.

Major discount stores sell much good tackle at reasonable prices, but their salespeople hardly ever have sufficient actual fishing experience to help you make the proper selection.

It is better for the beginner to buy his gear at a legitimate tackle store, even if he has to pay a higher price.

The advantages of shopping at a legitimate sporting goods store are many. First of all, the buyer of the store's tackle is acutely aware of his chain-store competition. He will not sell shoddy merchandise, or so-called bargain tackle, since he has to stake his reputation on happy customers who will come back again and again. He will also stock tackle to suit the fishing of the particular region and locale where he does business.

He offers personalized service. He'll wind line on the reel and splice a fly line to the backing, usually at no cost. He'll make line loops and tie special leaders. Usually he has a big selection of flies and fly-rod lures and knows, because of his intimate association with his customers, which patterns are catching fish.

Usually he is an officer of a local rod-and-gun or fishing club, and/or one of the fly-tying or fly-casting instructors, and he will be able to select tackle that's balanced and instruct the user in any new or advanced techniques of casting and presentation.

Usually he's a fisherman himself, and knows where to go and when and with what. He makes it his business to see to it that his customers come in to thank him for his advice and counsel. Talking with him during the quieter hours at the store will often reveal a lifetime of fishing experiences and much lore of the area.

The tackle store is where hunters and fishermen love to congregate and "shoot the breeze." There's a feeling of brotherhood. From these meetings will come new friendships and valuable interchanges of information, plus some good stories of fish that got away.

There is usually a nucleus of old timers who have been fishing in the area for many years. Many hints and tips can be garnered from these types just by listening and prodding them with questions.

The tackle store is a fount of catalog information. It's wise to keep up with the latest tackle developments, and catalogs are usually available just for the asking, for you to thumb through and ask questions about.

The tackle stores are humming with information about fish stocking programs, conservation projects, and law changes. Many of these shops issue fishing licenses, and have details on the legal aspects of fishing in their state. . . .

Visit and revisit your local tackle store. You'll profit by it.

Approaching and
Wading the Stream

Some years ago I was in a group of outdoor writers invited to the
Bahamas to act in a special promotion film on bonefishing. We
were invited because we were thought to be pretty good anglers—
and many of us had taken quite a few bonefish in our careers.

We were fishing a run between two reefs that almost joined
together between two islands. The tide was running and the water
in front of me looked like a wide trout stream, except it was so
gin-clear it often seemed the area was without water altogether.
Only a few current ripples told you there was any water there at all.

My guide and I were in a small rowboat and he was polling
me very slowly toward the tide rip so I could flycast to the bonefish that should be there on that tide. We'd pause, look, and proceed nearer the run.

The guide spotted them first. Six good bonefish in a V forma-
tion were gently and slowly cruising along the flats in about three
feet of water.

As I was about to cast my guide whispered for me to hold up.
"Wait 'til they start feeding or you'll spook 'em," he warned.

One of the fish paused and poked his nose down into the sand and the others followed.

"Now make your cast," my guide ordered.

I stood up in the boat, slowly, deliberately, and very carefully.

In an instant all the fish disappeared and it was ten minutes before any came into view again!

A similar lesson was learned from my perch on the bridge above the famous town pool on the Esopus, a fine Catskill stream where I've spent many years developing theories and gathering fodder for books.

I was standing there with Dick Fulkert, a fine fisherman and an even better fly tyer, and the bright sunlight was coming at an angle that made the water downstream from us an open book.

Two anglers were working the bottom of the pool, and two more were preparing to enter the smooth water at mid-pool.

As we scanned the water we spotted several of the big rainbows that can usually be found in that pool, having come up from the Ashokan Reservoir on their way to spawn.

The angler on the right side of the pool started to wade in. He hadn't yet put both feet in the water when those big rainbows—far away from him and under cover of about two feet of water—bolted for the deeper water below.

That's all it took to put them down.

So learn to approach the water quietly and carefully. And when you wade, wade *slowly.* You should move at a rate of about five feet per minute—and twice as slowly if you're fishing as you wade.

Wade *out of the way,* as far from the fishing lanes as you can get. Walk on land whenever possible. Wear dark clothes and try not to wave your arms or rod. If your rod has a shiny ferrule, tape it or paint it to cut down on the reflection.

Also, you must learn to approach the water *from the right spot.* Don't just go wading in where you expect to begin fishing.

Always look over the general area of water you are about to encounter, even if it's an old friend. Decide how you're going to start fishing. If the part of the stream you're considering is a long pool, for example, it would be a good idea (if you're going to fish down) to walk the length of the pool first, watching the water as you go, to see if there are any signs of action. Take up a position above the first water to be fished and work the water from the shore, casting into the shallows, working your way out gradually and fishing down slowly, *wading as little as possible.*

If you're planning on fishing upstream it makes sense to cruise all the way down to the bottom of the stretch where the water flattens out. There you can enter the waste water and not disturb anything above you. Or you might choose to rollcast from the shore and perhaps enter the water farther up.

Too many anglers just head straight for the water, wade out into it (usually disturbing the entire pool), and then wonder why they don't get any action. They wade where they should fish, and so miss the action and spoil it for others.

The angler should start casting from the point at which he is about to enter the water, even if it's only a ritual to get his tackle organized and his casting in order. Chances are he'll be able to fish the entire pool from shore, then wade in from below and wade up the middle, slowly and carefully, affording himself twice the opportunity for sport.

In the early part of the season, when there are many anglers working the water, it's a safe bet that the trout in any given stretch of fishable water will have been disturbed since before daylight and will remain hidden all day long until the angling hord retreats. This makes fishing a maddening proposition. I've seen times when a hatch is just beginning and a cluster of anglers immediately wades in casting frantically. Obviously this puts the trout off their feed and the area is ruined for the day. . . .

Look at all those guys wading and casting.

They're all at the head of the pool, aren't they?

Now all that wading disturbs the bottom, and the nymphs and larvae don't like that, so they take off and drift down-current. . . .

Take up a position well below. Load your leader with three nymphs. Drop them at your feet and feed out line so they drift naturally in the current below you.

Move quietly and slowly upstream and you'll have trout rising to drifting flies right under your rod tip—or hear them rising behind you in your wake.

Meanwhile, all those folks elbow-to-elbow upstream continue

How would you wade this pool? Well, before you leap in take a long look. You can walk up under the shade of those trees on the left and peer into the water to locate the hot spots you'll want to work. Since it would be foolhardy to enter the water from the bank under the trees, you'll have to walk down to A. Immediately above you is a cool, deep, gravelly run under the trees. Don't wade it. Enter at A and follow the dotted line. It's easy to cast in under the trees as you go along, throwing upstream mends to allow your flies to drift down and under the overhangs. Sometimes it may be necessary to cast laterally rather than vertically. Wading up the center you can work the other side of the pool too. At the split in my road map you can go left or right. The water above is shallow but fast, so when you want to change from left to right, drop back to the fork in the road and then proceed.

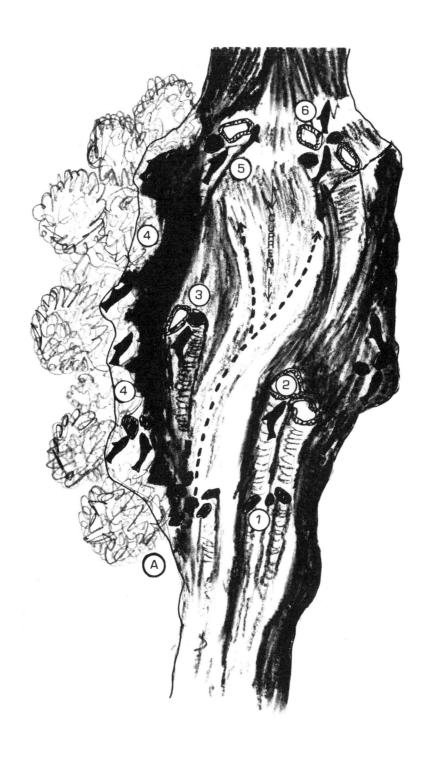

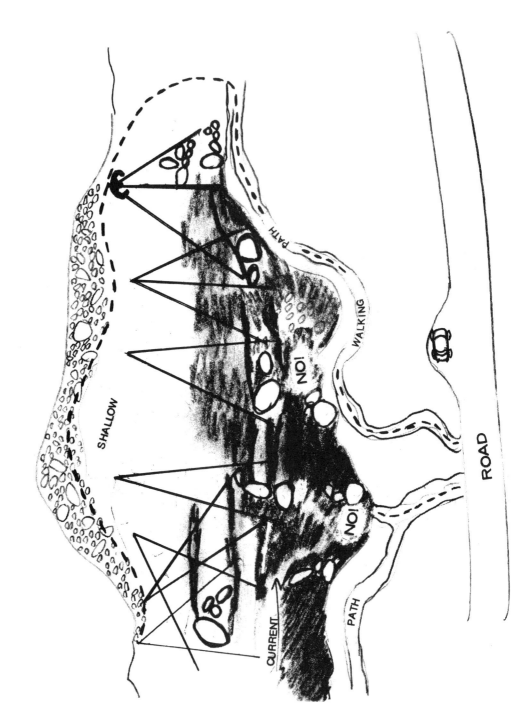

Your typical roadside pool.

Most anglers park their cars and blithely wade right in, entering the water wherever they happen to get to it. Wading where they ought to be fishing they are disturbing potential hot spots, like the areas where I've written NO!

Too bad for them!

Let's you and I walk downstream along the path, cross where there's waste water, and fish all that marvelous water on the road-side of the stream from the far shallows.

Bet we get something worth photographing!

to wade back and forth stirring up the bottom nymphs and larvae that drift down to entice your trout for you!

A good hard look at the contour of the water—its currents, eddies, soft glassy stretches, and white water—will offer clues as to your best entrance strategy, and will also pave the way to a commonsense approach to the style of fishing to be done.

This kind of prep work may show you that wading is unnecessary! Remember, in any given water there are combinations of little streams, short runs, undercut ledges, underwater holes, obstructions, gravelly stretches, and sudden drop-offs that can be cast to from shore—or maybe just a few feet out.

Just for kicks, someday make believe you are not dressed in your waders and approach the stream as if you could only wet your feet. Begin casting and work all the water within a comfortable casting distance. You'll be surprised how much fishing you'll get in, and, incidently, how much action will come about. Too many anglers concentrate on "out there" while the trout are nursing the rocks and snags of the shoreline.

I must tell you about the time four of us who have fished together for years parked the car midway along a half-mile stretch of the Esopus. Here the big river makes a right-angle turn amid some house-sized boulders, crashes down mightily for a few yards, then quickly flattens out in a long, deep pool that is deepest right in the center.

Along the far bank it is shady after noontime, thanks to some great old pines and oaks that drape their branches over the stream edge. Along that shoreline the water becomes quite shallow at times, the current fanning out to short stretches of fine gravel and sand.

The near side, next to the road, is boulder-banked with a little foliage in places offering shade and insect housing, and a thin narrow run that bubbles along as a fan-off from the main current.

We got out of the car and spread out along the top of the bank to get a look at the entire stretch. Apparently there were no hatches, and aside from a minnow or two rising out in the center, the stream was quiet.

In a few minutes we became restless and paced back and forth, eyes glued to the water for some sign.

Finally one of the quartet decided he couldn't wait any longer. He walked halfway down the bank and cast a brace of wet flies into the little side-current cascading right under the streamside brush. His first cast snagged a nice young alder, and he went down to extricate his flies. He dropped them into the water and raised his rod tip to guide them down the current. A bright flash of water and he was onto a nice little brown trout. He hooked it and released it and recast. It wasn't long before he had another . . . and another. . . .

We watched in awe. Ordinarily we would have waded right through that stretch of shoreline water and worked the deep!

Those of you fortunate enough to have experienced a swimming session in a lake or pond—or the deep hole of a stream—have probably learned that when you swim underwater and knock two stones together you hear a loud click in your ear. (If some smart guy did this too close to you your ear ached for quite a spell!)

Well imagine, if you will, the grinding sound of gravel and small pebbles when you take a step in the water. Magnify that sound by a *pair* of booted feet constantly grinding the bottom, and then imagine about five or *six* people doing this!

No wonder trout become paranoid!

The first consideration in wading is to learn to *walk*, not just stomp or plod along as most of us do, oblivious of the terrifying underwater noise we are creating. In learning how to wade so as to keep down the sound level, we are also learning how best to balance ourselves and proceed with more ease—and safety.

It is one thing to walk along a river's edge and pound down hard for secure footing, or to pick one's way daintily between the bigger rocks in order not to rub one's waders against stone unnecessarily. . . .

Enter into the world of water, however, and the scene changes into something quite different. No matter how keenly you peer down it is going to be increasingly hard, and eventually impossible, for you to see your feet and plan by sight where you are going to take your next step. The problem is the same in the gin-clear water of the Bahama flats or a high-elevation western trout stream. Look down and you are unable to judge depth. Your next step may be a foot below your present position.

So, common sense would dictate the first rule of safe wading to be FEEL THE BOTTOM WITH YOUR FEET.

Don't just step ahead blindly. You could twist an ankle, bruise a shinbone, slide off an unsteady rock and bust your elbow or step into a hole.

By *feeling your way* I mean that you should try and keep your toe and heel in touch with whatever is ahead and under you. As you lift your foot to make the next move, don't just raise it up and slap it down ahead of you. Drag it across whatever is there. Test. You can quickly and easily adjust—or withdraw. If you feel a big rock and don't want to put your foot on it, slide your foot over it, down, and around, until you find a firm setting. Then move your other foot using the same routine.

Make only short moves, keeping your weight on the back foot until your front foot is secure.

Wading a trout stream need never be any more dangerous than crossing an icy street. You walk cautiously, keeping your balance and not moving forward until you know what you are moving *on*.

Let me warn you that there are rocks that have been put in trout streams in a very special way. They've been poised there just to harrass anglers. They are neatly balanced so that at the placement of your foot, they will instantly roll over and if you are not careful you will roll with them.

So be careful. Move little-by-less, slithering along the bottom and knowing where your next staunch footing is going to be before you put your full weight on it.

When you wish to proceed through fast current, be it a foot deep or as high as your belt, wade sideways, moving each foot only inches at a time and keeping your body arched against the current with your knees bent for spring balance when needed.

It takes a little longer to do it this way but it pays off.

When you wade sideways the current affects you with half the intensity it would if you were to face it head on. If you have ever been swimming in the surf you should know this by experience. When a wave is about to break near your shoulder, you merely shove your shoulder into it, stick your elbow out at it, and slice the impact of the water in half. The wave slides by rather than knocking you over.

Keep in mind where you're going and why, and how to return if you need to. Quite often by taking what looks like the easier route you lead yourself into a trap. When you get to the end it's too deep to continue and there's no exit to the left or right. Now what? Wade your way back? Brother that is going to be hard— some of the hardest minutes you've ever spent. It's one thing to angle *against* the current and keep your balance. With the current *behind* you however, the pressure is going to be quite unnatural, and each step you take is going to be a terror.

This situation can arise when you are wading downstream in the center and suddenly you find that the reef you're on is falling off: one more step and you'll be in over your wader tops! You're only a few feet from the bank but the water between you and the shore is twice as fast now and impossible for you to challenge.

What do you do?

You turn around and face the current and see the many feet back upstream you'll have to travel. By the way, before you start back up, break your rod down and use the shortest length as a balance. Button all your jacket pockets and pull your hat on tight.

. . .

I'll give you a few minutes to return while I watch from the bank.

Suppose you're wading a stream like the Au Sable (in New York State) in May. This is a rough trip. The rocks are very slimy —soapstone to begin with and covered with a thick film of slime. The bottom is made up of long slick rock ledges, on some of which I've actually slid while trying to stand still, much less take a step!

A wading staff is a must here. Try a cut-down broom handle or a discarded ski pole without the basket. The pole should be attached to a leather cord and this clipped to your belt. It will drag behind you but be instantly available when you need it, so long as the slack line you gathered in from last cast is not woven around it by the current.

Chains are an added aid to wading under gravelly conditions, but they also make an additional percussion and can be heard by

A shows how to sidestep at an angle to the current. It's much easier to inch your way upstream this way rather than facing the current directly. Move your feet just a bit at a time.

B shows how to pick your way between rocks that are too large to step over or that might roll with your weight. Instead of stepping, feel the bottom with your feet and do not put your weight on the forward foot until you are secure.

C shows how to go across-stream. Instead of trying to cross ahead of the rocks, where the current's much stronger, make your crossing in the rocks' wake.

All else being equal, broken water is always *slower.*

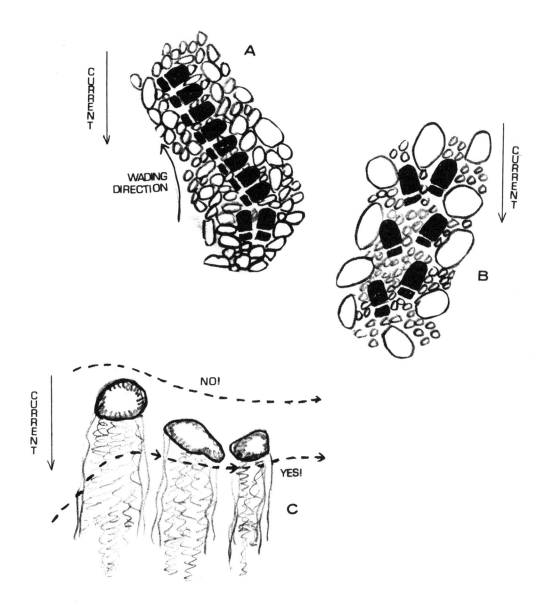

A

CURRENT

WADING
DIRECTION

B

CURRENT

C

CURRENT

NO!

YES!

the trout even before you make a move, so I recommend foregoing chains unless you feel they're absolutely necessary.

Remember, with enough casting tricks in your control you can avoid wading much of the time and should. You'll find that wading in most cases is entirely unnecessary, or at least that it can be done with a minimum of effort and water disturbance. You'll find ways to save your feet and use your casting arm instead. You'll be wading where you should wade and fishing where you should fish.

And cutting down your wading will help the aquatic insects on your stream. When you're plodding along in their environment you're walking all over them, dislodging them, killing them . . . multiply this by hundreds of anglers over a given stretch and it's no wonder our mayflies and other aquatic insects are becoming less and less present.

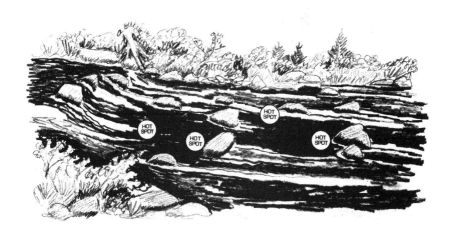

Calling Your Shots

At the risk of repeating myself I want to impress you with the necessity of planning out your tactics before you start fishing any given stretch of stream.

All too often we have the tendency as we wade along to cast just anywhere without any specific idea in mind. An improvement might be to begin to think like a pool shark. Call your shots. Pick your hot spots and concentrate on them. Cast with a specific purpose and intent. Wade as little as possible, and when you do wade, remember that it's better to approach your hot spots from the side rather than mid-stream.

Before you start fishing spend a few minutes looking at the water, noting its current flows, backwashes, eddies, sluices, surfy waters and calm, glassy stretches. You'll begin to visualize just how your flies are going to act in various situations. You'll learn where and where not to cast. You'll discover ways to cast above a given hot spot, or how to approach it from the side. You'll begin to formulate tactics of presentation. Pre-planning may not pay off all the time, but you will catch more fish on the average, and, armed with a purpose, a tactic to try, and a specific stream area in which you will strive to make your flies act as they should, you will find fishing more *interesting*.

Let's look at an example.

You're fishing dry, working your way upstream toward a pair of rocks near the head of a pool. Between these rocks is a shallow bridge of gravel and sand. The current is fairly strong, and the water is about two feet deep behind the rocks and even deeper above them.

You look forward to casting to those rocks, the washes below them, and also the water immediately above them.

This whole area is your hot spot.

Instead of proceeding dead ahead upstream and casting directly upstream to the first area you want to cover (the washes below the rocks) however, you do a little thinking and a little planning before making your move.

You start upstream by wading quietly to the side. In this way you'll be able to present your flies so that on the downstream float the drifting line won't put down fish in your hot-spot area.

You make your casts toward the water slightly above the dead-water area above the rock. The first casts will land on your side of the rock, about four or five feet away from it. This is not the hot spot yet. You are simply testing the water for drift and feel.

With your rod held high, the fly will drift naturally for a foot or two, and then drag will set in. As it does, you have two options: pick it up and cast again or throw a loop of line up ahead of the cast to allow the fly to drift drag-free a bit further.

Now when that fly drifts down below the rock, allow it to swing very slowly on the currents—feeding line to it to slow the drift across the water—until it drops below you. On the retrieve, skitter it in when it gets to the stream edge. If there are deep holes there, there is always a possibility.

Now you're ready really to concentrate on the hot spot, having mastered casting distance, drift technique, mending, and retrieve. You're going to go for those few feet above the first rock. So make your first cast well above the rock and mend a loop of free line so your fly will drift naturally as it reaches to within a couple of feet of the rock. Instead of picking up the fly for a recast, you rollcast it out a couple of feet more so it now sits on the far side of and above the rock. It drifts down almost to the rock and you pick it up and immediately drop it back down in front of the rock and let the current take it right around the edge. Throw additional line to it and allow it to drift down into the rock wash and ride right along the wavelets made by the rock. Don't pick it up for a recast. Roll that fly right back to your side of the rock and let it drift. Finally, skitter it across both above and below.

You can work this same area that we've been talking about from above. Wade ashore from where you are, enter from above, and drop your fly into the water well above the rock. Pay out slack until your fly reaches the two-foot area below the rock and then rollcast a pickup and set the fly down upstream a bit and let it drift down again. Allow the fly to ride both sides of both rocks and on down into the wakes.

If the dry fly doesn't get you a tumble, try the same routine with a pair of nymphs or slim wet flies. If these don't work, tie on a small bucktail and whale the devil out of that area.

Don't ever be afraid to work an area thoroughly. Take your time. Pause between casts. Take the time to change from wet fly to dry. Try different patterns and sizes.

Too often we have the tendency to give up WHEN WE KNOW THERE ARE TROUT IN THERE. Our restlessness moves us on to fresh stretches. We fish in kind of a casual way, dropping our flies indiscriminately into the pockets and hot spots without any pre-planning or follow-up. And chances are we go home without very much action to tell about.

Try this for size:

The time is early in the season. The hatchery trout planted some weeks ago have already begun to feed naturally on stream insects. Those trout taken so far have been filled almost to the gullet with larvae and nymphs.

Due to much wading and disturbance of the stream bottom, many nymphs are dislodged and drifting free in the current. There are some of the swimming type too.

Under these circumstances one of the most productive presentation techniques is what I call the *controlled rise retrieve.*

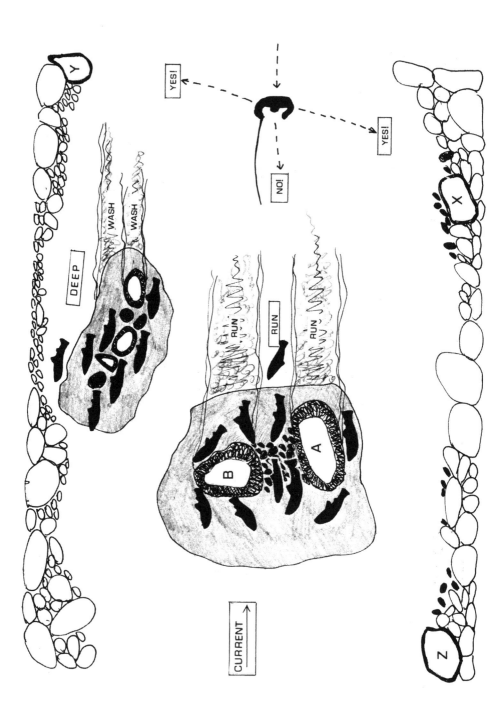

You're approaching from below. The pair of center rocks dominates the pool. That's your hot spot. You move upstream slowly, not pushing any water ahead of you, and start making gentle casts to the washes. Your real hot spot will be just upstream of the rocks, in the deeper, faster current that is broken by them.

Don't wade up the middle! Go ashore, or as close to it as you can get without losing your casting range (X would be ideal), and start placing your casts carefully. Work your casts farther and farther up until you're at last hitting the hot water above the rocks. Even though you're fishing almost directly upstream, throw a curved line so your fly (or flies) will drift down naturally to, and below, the rock (on your side of it). Then you work the middle, and finally rock B, where you'll rollcast a nice wide curve cast, raising your rod tip to let the line run, or flipping it over rock A and retrieving gently.

Later you can fish this stretch from above (Z), drifting your flies right to the water in front of the rocks. Let 'em sink (if you're using nymphs), and then raise 'em up right at the hot spot—the front of the rocks—and dapple.

A lesser but still worthwhile hot spot is the rock cluster on the right. You can't reach this area from your first approach, so you hike downstream and cross over below and work your way back up to Y.

IMPORTANT: Before you start casting to whatever hot spot you've chosen, decide where, if you hook onto a fish, you want to fight it. Pre-plan your strategy, taking into account what snags and fallen trees and underwater weeds your catch might try to hang you up in, and locating that section of quieter water, away from your hot spot, you want to play your catch into. This way, when the hit comes you'll be ready.

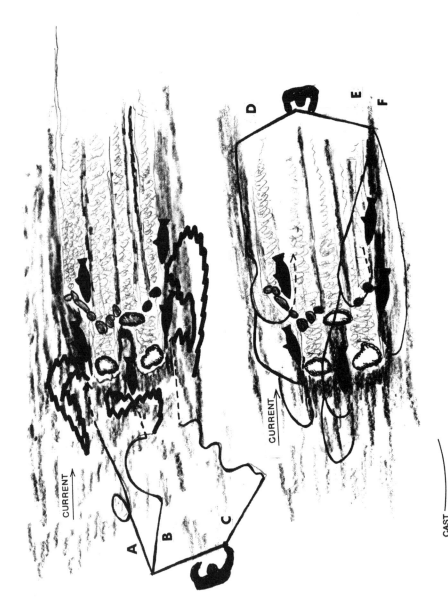

CURRENT

CURRENT

A

B

C

D

E

F

CAST ——————
DRIFT ------------
RETRIEVE ∿∿∿∿∿∿

You're fishing downstream and come upon a cluster of rocks—nothing fancy but well worth trying. As you approach the hot spot you move slightly to the side. Choosing a bucktail you make your first cast (A), pulling back lightly and then immediately letting out some line and letting the fly drift. As it approaches the rocks you call your shot and begin activating it, working it back toward you as shown.

Your next try is dead center. To sink your fly deep you drop it with a wide arc of line (B), which should be absorbed as the fly drifts down. Retrieve in very short jerks, allowing the fly to drop down again and again, almost like a fore-and-aft spinner plug.

Your approach to the near side of the rock cluster uses the stop cast (C) and dead drift. The fly drops below the rock and flows gently down the deep side of the wash. Activate it as shown, retrieve, and repeat.

Approaching from below you throw loop casts, or better, roll-and-mend curves, targeting your fly (or flies) to come down just above the hot spot and then letting them drift down.

This presentation covers the water from the bottom up, maximizing its effectiveness just as your fly (or flies) reach the hot spot where you want the action to come off.

Face directly downstream, preferably with a main current run to one side. Drop your weighted flies with slack line and feed them out as the current dictates. When they are about thirty feet below you, gently raise your rod tip, causing them to surface. The second you see them, release some more line and lower your rod tip to let them sink and drift for about ten more feet.

This is one of the most effective presentation methods I know for fish hunting, especially in the early high-water season.

Use it when calling your shots over a particular break in the current or just below the lip of a pool that you can cast to from above.

It is very effective too at the tail of a pool where the current begins to break just before the pool's bottom lip. Trout will rest there waiting for insects to drop down to them. In this case you have to wade very quietly since they can see you coming. It's best to approach from the side, casting your flies directly across and letting them sink down slowly on the drift. At just the point where the water begins to flow over the lip of the pool, raise your rod and strip in a little line. The rising action of the nymph will be natural and any action now should be an explosion.

This same technique is also good during the days of the hatches. The nymphs leave the bottom and either drift or swim for quite a long time in the midstream current. If a hatch is going to appear at about noon, try this drift presentation at about eleven. If you're observant you'll see nymphs drifting in the current about a foot below the surface. Match this action. Call your shot just ahead of a stream snag, submerged rock, or sudden rise of the bottom. That's where you want your flies suddenly rising to the surface.

Quite often the hit will not take place underwater. The fish will wait until your fly is on or very near the surface.

This same technique can be used when you're bucktailing. Sink the fly well and let it drift on a slack line until it reaches the hot-spot point where you expect your strike. Again, you want the action to come off at the exact spot where you expect a trout to be lying in wait. When you think your fly is near the targeted point, raise your rod tip. Up to the surface comes your fly. . . .

If you don't get an immediate strike, drop your fly down on slack line and raise it up again and skitter it.

When the fly has run its course and your cast is well below you, work it back to you in very short jerks. If the water is a foot or so deep you can spend a good bit of time fishing your fly back to you, especially in water where the current is not so strong.

Recast and repeat the process over the same water you've been working. Those trout are hanging out down there among those current breaks just waiting for your fly to come floating down toward them and then suddenly rise surfaceward like a lifting nymph. If you can call your shot to get the rise to occur just a foot or so upstream of your quarry's nose, you'll most likely be in business.

When They're Hitting Light

There's nothing quite so exasperating as a trout that hits light and misses your fly. . . .

You're fishing near the head of a pool, working upstream with dries. Your longest cast falls conveniently short of where the current is lashing down out of the white water above. Your fly settles on the surface exactly where you intended it to, a few feet below where the current slows to form fingers of wash lines which eventually mingle with the quieter water.

You see trout splashing the surface, actively feeding. A few insects are in the air—and some in the film and on the water surface. There's a hatch on, either here or further upstream: prime time.

As your dry fly rides gracefully among the bubbles and drifting naturals, you watch your slack, ready for the strike. . . .

BANG!

He missed. You throw a cast right back in there for another shot. Several trout rise at once, and one goes for your fly—but misses . . . the same thing happens again, and again. . . .

What's wrong?

Well, there can be more than one answer. And while those trout are up there having a ball you'd better calm down and think through the possibilities of what could be happening.

Look carefully at the fish as they feed. Are they really taking flies off the surface or is what you're seeing the tailing of trout feeding *under* the surface—or bulging—taking insects that are floating along just a bit under the surface film?

If they're feeding under the film—probably on washings or hatched flies that have been pummelled by the fast currents above —your high-floating dry with its stiff hackle probably wasn't even seen. The rise you thought was to *it* was most likely to something else.

So your first thought is to try another pattern that will possibly match the naturals. You switch several times, but with no results.

So now, a commonsense approach. You decide to tie on a fly that will lie in the film half submerged, figuring that the trout didn't see your high floater well enough to make him strike with gusto. This fly isn't easy for you to see, but what's the difference if it works?

You might try the one design that has worked for me in fast water, rough currents, and especially at the heads of pools where a combination of flies coming down from the white water above is mingling with a hatch or near hatch.

It's the downwing dry fly. This is a killer that too many of us have had little experience with simply because we think of dry flies as having upright wings.

Are those mayflies the trout are taking? Or is there a mixture of caddis on the water? We all know caddis bend their wings back over their bodies. If it's a hatch of caddis those fish are after, the wings aren't upright at all.

Far too much attention has been given to the mayfly. The caddis and landbreds far outnumber them in variety and size all season long on most streams. In many of our streams where the mayfly hatches are disappearing, the caddis seems to make out very well, and in some streams is actually on the increase. Caddis hatch in veritable droves. Clouds of them cover the water. Sure there may be mayflies among them, but you can bet they aren't riding high. They're partially submerged—particularly if they've been driven through the white water above. If hatching, they will be found riding in the film until their pupal case is thoroughly discarded, a process that takes quite a while as they drift along at the mercy of the current.

The situation would argue for the downwing fly. Try a Quill Gordon, Hendrickson, March Brown, or Green Drake, for starters, in sizes 16 to 20.

Possibility two: You're casting upstream-and-across, throwing a mend upstream to avoid drag on the first part of the downstream drift. This means slack is present. But those rises are sudden and quick. The trout are going for the fly (yours or a natural) with a circular rise that peaks just at the surface. They are not deliberately and slowly rising on an angle to suck the fly in as they do in slower water. But making the sudden, rushing type of rise they can easily miss. Either the fly is bumped by the trout's nose or else taken in and rejected in a thousandth of a second (and boy can they do it!). Your reactive strike is virtually *always* too late, and unless they accidently hook themselves you have what you think was a light hit.

There are two remedies. The first is to try to eliminate the slack more quickly after your fly hits the water so that when you react to a hit the time-lapse is reduced. If the water is tumbly enough there is no need for the upstream bend. The trout aren't going to be put down if you draw the slack in immediately after the cast. You might try falsecasting your fly over the target area and on the drop-down pulling back just a little to assure a straight line and leader. Another trick is the very opposite: you use a wide upstream loop cast. The loop will act as a bobber. Watch the line as well as the fly and the instant you see either move, *strike*.

The second remedy involves the diameter of your leader. Most of us like to use the finest tippet possible when dry-fly fishing. But in heavy water a superfine tippet may well be too soft and limp. In fact you're better off using a heavier leader. It will be easier to control your slack and also to strike more quickly and decisively.

If you're like me, you're lazy. The possibility that changing your rig might help seldom occurs to you. Changing our leader and fly takes time, and those trout are out there and we want action, so we go on using what we've been using and fish after fish is missed. But consider changing—in this case to a heavier tippet (with the same fly), or else a size heavier leader and a one-size-larger fly.

A third solution to contemplate (we're still at the head of that pool and haven't hooked a trout yet!) relates to casting position. You've been approaching from the classical downstream location, casting straight up or partially so. Wade ashore now. Move upstream and rollcast your fly across the water to the first basic current run and let it settle in the current. As it does, throw a three- or four-foot loop of line upstream of the leader and watch it like a bobber. You may get a strike to the fly that you cannot see. Any sudden movement of that slack line will alert you. The added line above will also act as a drag—just enough to resist a strike and help set the hook. Note also that you are in much better control now. Casting from this new position you're able to make your response quicker and more deadly.

Now extend your cast across the stream, or into the next current slick, and allow the upstream line to be absorbed. . . .

As an extreme possibility (against the old-school orthodoxy), why not take a position *above* the area you've been working? Cast across and slightly downstream—yes, with the dry fly—throwing an upstream loop again to act as a bobber (and also offer absorption time before the fly is dragged under by the current). From this position you can either rollcast or use the conventional fore-and-aft cast, stopping the flow of line just above the area to be worked and allowing your fly to drop down. Use a soft-hackled pattern that will ride the surface film, or the spentwing or downwing. These will be harder for you to see of course, but the trout will see them and that is the point of the exercise.

There's another possible cure for short hits, and it involves the length of your cast. Most of us have the desire to reach out there fifty to sixty feet or more. It looks pretty and we love to perform. But at that distance it's practically impossible to connect to a light hit. So don't try to reach the other shore with a long cast you can't control.

Concentrate on the water close to you. You might just pick

The fish on the left is tailing. He's feeding on nymphs. Or, if the water's shallow enough and there's aquatic vegetation, he may be rutting in the underwater grasses looking for bugs.

The next trout is coming to the surface with an obvious mouthful of fresh-caught nymph. He's not at all interested in the Mayfly right next to him.

The third trout is rolling. He may be taking nymphs as they hit the surface, or possibly what you're seeing is the follow-through of a rise from the bottom to take nymphs several inches under.

The fact is, it's all conjecture. No one really knows at any given moment what's going on under there. Your fly may be rejected because it's the wrong pattern, because it's the wrong size, because it's drifting at the wrong level, because it's moving too quickly (or slowly), because the trout can't see it, because they can see you, or for any number of other reasons.

All you can do is observe—pay constant and close attention to what you see around you on the water, under it, and in the air (and in the stomach of the fish you've caught and kept)—and hope you can come up with the right combination of pattern and presentation.

If you're having trouble, make yourself stop fishing and just watch the water for a while. If eventually you're lucky enough to have your eyes on a particular insect when a trout busts it, you can assume you now know what he wants. And remember, there needn't always be a splash—or even a dimple. If you're watching a Mayfly ride downstream and suddenly it disappears without even a ring, 10 to 1 a big trout inhaled it.

up a good one right under your rod tip. The trout are not nearly so scared here as they will be below, in the quiet stretches. There's plenty of pool. Leave the long shots alone and concentrate on the area close at hand. Cast and then keep your rod pointed high with all of the line out of water right to the leader knot. Use a shorter leader than you would on the flats and a heavier tippet, as suggested before.

Go armed with a longer rod. Short rods are fun, but the longer stick with a stiff tip will help overcome your slack quicker. Try a big old nine-footer, especially if you're a shorty and hip-deep in water.

Now. Suppose those trout are still feeding up ahead of you and you still can't stay hooked to one. Try a set-up our fathers used when we were young: two wet flies on a tapered 4X leader. Make casts of 30 feet. Hold your rod high, with all the line out of the water, and gently skitter the flies over the surface, right across the currents, back and forth. When you've retrieved them in close roll-cast them right back out again and rework the area. WHAMMO! When they hit you'll know it for sure.

Okay you try all this and *still* don't connect. Tie on a bucktail, take up a position quartering and above the area, and starting from the very edge of the stream work your casts out over those runs, starting where the white water is just dispersing down into the wider and slower currents.

Drop that fly. Throw a loop of leader ahead of it so it will sink a bit, then in very short jerks work the fly back to you up and across the runs. The trout may well be feeding on specific insects, but seeing your "minnow" a big trout just might become inflamed. . . .

Really there's no such thing as a light or short hit. It's a miss, and you missed because you weren't fast enough on the draw, or the trout wasn't rising to your fly anyway because he couldn't see it—or it was skidding by too fast—or he made a split-second last-minute decision he didn't want it.

The "light-hit" problem is not known only to dry-fly fishermen. It occurs frequently with nymphs and for some very good reasons. It has been driven into our heads that we must dead-drift nymphs on a slack line so they'll flow naturally with the current.

Consequently we tend to cast our nymphs slightly upstream and across, allowing them to sink to a depth at which we hope a trout will see them and strike.

Now this is a vague proposition at best. Even though it works some of the time, it's still a chuck-and-chance-it way of handling one's flies. If we get a good strike and the fish hooks itself we consider we're on the right track. But more often than not the trout that is not actively feeding on rising nymphs will nose the fly, bump it, taste it suspectingly, and reject. But if we're fishing across and downstream, dead-drift style, many a trout will take advantage of our slack line to taste our fly and reject it without our knowing it. So in plain English we're fishing blind.

Fly tyers have come up with a pretty good answer in the weighted nymph. However, we theorize that a weighted nymph is going to act unnaturally in the water, so we pinch split shot or wrap-around lead onto our leader, ahead of our fly or flies, and this tends to sink them without affecting their natural flow in the current.

But the split shot can snag unmercifully on the bottom rocks and gravel, so badly so, sometimes, that we have to break our rig off and start all over again. But we do have to get those nymphs down deep if we want to connect . . . so let's experiment. . . .

The following trick was learned by sheer accident. It's one of the best ways of sinking nymphs I know—and without a lot of excess slack. I was fishing the Housatonic one time, in western Connecticut, and I had wrapped a strip of lead around my leader to get my nymphs down where I wanted them. Well, I snagged, and in struggling to unlock my leader from the rocks I was unknowingly (I later discovered) unwinding the lead strip, except at the very top. I began my retrieve, figuring that the lead was safely on as it had been originally tied, and gradually lowered the rod tip to allow the flies and their weight to drift deep below me. A trout struck, and when I got him in I noticed that my lead strip was hanging precariously by its very top edge. I unhooked the trout and recast without worrying about the lead. I figured that if it came off, I'd replace it on the next cast. Well, I fished for the next half hour with that lead just hanging there on my leader and I didn't get snagged once, even in the process of catching and unhooking several trout. REVELATION! Tie your lead on so most of it extends free of your leader and forget the split shot altogether. I've used this trick for years, even with big wet flies, and seldom become snagged. It seems the lead slithers somehow between the rocks and snags, enabling you to keep your flies drifting deep.

But suppose you've seen nymphs drifting fairly near the surface, preparatory to hatching in a few minutes or so, and you want to dead-drift your imitations in the usual unweighted manner. You're in for light hits for sure . . . but there are some ways to overcome them.

Conventional nymph fishing is generally done downstream or down and across. So let's work that way for a moment. Remembering that we use upstream bends and loops in dry-fly fishing, we can consider using the same techniques for under-the-surface drifting nymphs. Throw a loop of line upstream of your flies and use it as a bobber. Do the same with the across-and-upstream cast, and as your flies drift down in the current keep looping a bend of line upstream where you made the first cast. Repeat this several times and keep your eye on that line. Out across the water your nymphs are drifting back almost in line with you, but your line is still upstream of you if you have performed this correctly. Now, to fish your nymphs across and below you without recasting, allow the line that's upstream to be absorbed, and, at the last of it, turn your body to it and following its direction closely turn to a downstream position. When that bend of slack line is about opposite you, throw another loop of slack upstream of it and watch this absorb. Do this once more. By now your nymphs are quite a way downstream. But don't recast. Allow the nymphs to straighten out the line, and just as they begin to rise, because of the tension, swing the rod to the side of the stream so that they drift now across the current below you. As they do, throw a short rollcast of extra line and point your rod toward the bank at almost a right angle to the position of the nymphs. This will give you the bobber effect with the line and offer just enough resistance to enable you to feel a hit.

Nor are bucktail and streamer flies immune to short or light hits. The trout will bump them and nip at the feathers without seeming to want to take.

Cures?

First of all, streamers and bucktails should *never* be tied so that the feathers or fur extend beyond the bend of the hook. This

This is the downwing dry fly, at least the way I tie it. Conventional body as you like it. Caddis bodies are fuzzy, not clear and slick, so I use dubbing. Caddis don't have tails, but I put 'em on anyway, just for looks. The wings are made from duck flight-feather sections and are mounted backwards (versus the usual dry-fly mount) so that they curve down. The hackle is not thick, nor is it necessarily web-free. Use hen hackle—sparse, so the hook will sink and the body rest in the film. Tie these size 14–16 unless you're fishing the Montana high country, where the Caddis come in a size 10 in September.

unfortunately eliminates all store-bought flies. Sure they look pretty, and they do have an enticing action because of the feather-length. But they invite short and light hits. I know that streamers and bucktails have been taking big trout for years, and in many cases have taken consistently larger trout than have other fly types, but we are not concerned with the trout that hook themselves. We are concerned with light hits and how to overcome them. So use short flies, whether you have to burn or cut off the ends of the feathers or fur—or tie them all yourself.

Many will argue that trout seldom chase a minnow, but rather attack it from the front or side, so that feathers or fur extending

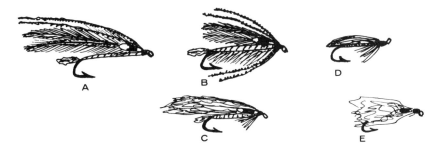

Shown at the left (A) is your everyday overdressed too-long fly. No wonder the short hits! B is better, yet still might lack vivacity in its action. C is clearly too long. The little guys on the right side, a salmon fly (D) and a killer Maribou (E), are more like it: tails not too long—not too cluttered up with paraphernalia.

beyond the hook bend are of no consequence. Not having seen enough trout strike at minnows I cannot state categorically that this is wrong. I do know, however, that I have had much better luck with the short flies, and I highly recommend them.

Another solution to light hits on streamers and bucktails would be the use of shorter, stiffer leaders. This point will be argued until dawn by some anglers who are adept with these flies, but I've found I can manipulate them much more to my liking when I have the added control a stiffer and shorter leader provides.

Also, I like to strike hard, and a leader that's too thin will snap.

As to presentation, I fish the streamer-bucktail in all directions, at times including straight upstream. Again, I use the extended loop of line and make it act as a bobber on the drift. I often fish these flies at right angles to my drifting line, continually rollcasting line way above the drifting fly.

These are just a few suggestions for curing light hits, and in using them you'll probably come up with some innovations of your own.

Don't be afraid to play around and experiment. Far too often anglers have the bad habit of mindlessly obeying rules they believe to be sacrosanct, when in fact they should be breaking loose and creating techniques of their own.

Where Are the Trout?

One of the reasons many of us do a lot of casting and not much catching is that we are unaware of where the fish are in relation to the stream bottom. Unless we have a pretty good idea of where they are—whether lying on the bottom or feeding on the surface—our casting and lure presentation will be pretty much "chuck and chance it."

So let's see if we can't get some idea of how to approach various stream situations. Let's first look briefly at the basic characteristics of the three best known types of trout: the brook, the brown, and the rainbow.

The broad streams of the Catskills, some of the Pennsylvania streams, and some of the New England streams offer long reaches of water where brown trout hold right out in the open. They are perfectly content to sit out there in the bright sunlight and feed on the surface from time to time in the bright light of day.

The brook trout, basically a fish of the smaller, shadier streams, will hold in close to the bank or on the bottom of a pool and seldom be found feeding on the surface. In the deep, cold Maine brooks and connecting streams between lakes I've seen

magnificent hatches of mayflies and caddis without the least si.
of a brookie busting the surface. Under the same conditions,
browns would be roiling the water and taking practically any dry
fly you offered, you can bet.

The rainbow likes the fastest parts of the stream and finds
rocks and holes to rest in, out of or under the current. Rainbows
will be found feeding in very fast water where the brown and certainly the brook trout seldom venture. This is one reason why
many techniques for fishing for brown trout are not successful in
our western streams.

The commonsense approach to fly fishing in your local waters,
then, would be to concentrate on observing the conditions at hand
and the habits of the particular species of trout you're fishing for.
There are, however, certain fixed rules that all trout obey and that
can be depended on. For instance, they don't like to work any
harder than necessary for their food and will tend to rest out of
the current as much as possible. Only when migrating or venturing
forth to feed will they put up with fast current. This will be only
for a short time and then they'll go back to their cozy corner either
down deep or underneath the fast current where you can't see
them.

As we look down on a stream we can't always see those
pockets in the current. We see just the fast water.

Broken white water is often shunned by the dry fly fisherman,
because it is impossible to float a dry fly on those fast moving
bubbles. But is he out to float flies or catch fish? There are trout
under that fast water. If you could get in under there you would
see that the flow is comparatively calm, and that given some holes
and/or dead spots to rest in, the fish will find this water attractive.

Another case: a slick pool with a slight current forming from
a sharp V. Obviously something is causing this, and sure enough,
when we look more closely at the situation we see that quite a few
feet upstream an underwater rock (or rise of the stream bottom) is
the cause of the change in the water flow.

Our tendency is to cast to the current break *as we perceive it*
(the V we see on the surface), thus missing the *real* hot spot, which
is that virtually dead area *ahead* of the underwater rock that's
causing the break. This calm water is where fish often like to hang
out, and should never be neglected.

Most anglers will pass up those stretches of water where there are no slicks and glides. These stretches are characterized by big boulders and fast, short runs where it's almost impossible to wade and likewise to cast a fly so it can be seen. Yet this is just the kind of water hatchery brook trout will gravitate to, and often rainbows too. When you flick your flies into those holes the strike will be instantaneous, so be ready to set that hook *fast.*

Underhangs in the curve of a stream are good places to work too. In most cases, however, these hot spots are simply cast to once or twice and the angler moves on. But the trout are in there, and they're big ones. Because of the nature of the current they stay flat against the wall under the overhang and will not venture out for anything that doesn't pass right by their nose. They're big because no one cares enough really to work for them, persisting until a float is achieved that gets the fly in under the bank and *close.*

Backwaters of pools are another prime location. But again, the trout are down deep, not fooling around on the surface unless there are a lot of insects in the film or a hatch is on. A casual cast to this type of water is usually a waste of time. Work it over well. And go *deep.*

Fishing for the brook trout in its native habitat you have to find the deepest holes in the stream and work them over thoroughly. Brook trout will not come to your nice glides over the flat water, and this is why the sunken wet fly and the streamer are such good flies for brookies.

Many of our best streams were once good brook trout waters, but they were fished out quickly by worm fishermen and spinner users. When logging and other practices caused the water to warm up, and the stream banks became devoid of natural foliage cover, these streams were dead—until the importation of the brown. Fishing today on our best Eastern streams is tops thanks to the brown trout and its ability to live in open, sun-drenched stretches of water.

On the pages that follow I give you some sample stream situations and show you how you can expect fish to act under the particular conditions described. Study these and remember them your next time out. You'll find the experience of fishing more interesting, and you'll catch more fish!

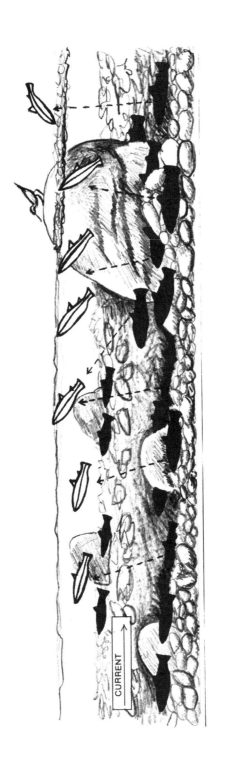

A cross-section of bumpy bottom with the trout laying low, resting between feedings. Note that they can find refuge behind even a small incline. They rest like this most of the time. If there's no definite hatch coming off—only a few insects drifting by over the fish's heads—they'll leave the bottom to snap at their food and promptly descend back to their original resting place.

Note that most of the fish have sought out a rock to hang by . . . note moreover that more fish rest alongside or even up-current of their rock than do in the downstream wake.

That trout inevitably hang out in the washes of rocks, and are seldom found alongside or just up-stream, is a myth that has lost countless anglers countless moments of pleasure.

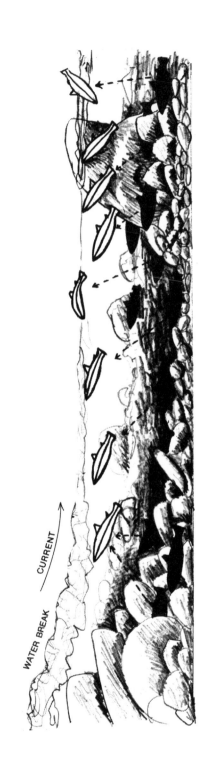

The head of a pool complete with waterbreak and center rock.

Note that the trout hugging the big boulders at the head of the pool are resting quite comfortably under all that fast water whizzing over their heads.

When it comes time to feed however, they'll drop back downstream a bit and surface, hanging there with their noses at whatever level food's to be found.

The trout near the center rock hug it closely while they're resting. When they see the insects they want, whether in the current or on the surface, they leave their resting place and rise into action.

A shelving riffle. The backwater at the upper left is a holding place for trout. They'll sit there on the bottom and rise only to the hatch—sometimes not then.

The deep run is where the majority will hang out, since the water on the riffle is difficult: shallow and fast.

So don't wade the deep run. Fish from the edges on either side. If possible don't wade at all.

When a hatch begins to come down those trout in the deep run will move up to the very lip of the riffle and hang there, scooping up anything from tiny midges to big land-bred blow-ins.

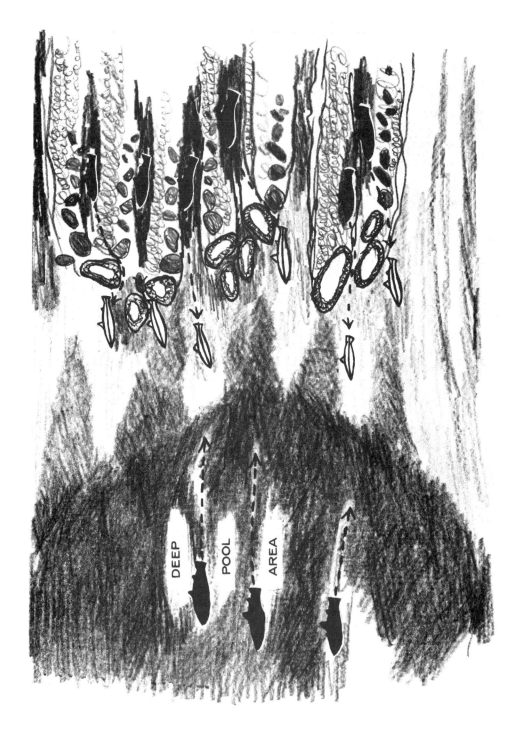

The tail of a deep pool. The hot spot lies be-tween the end of the deep water and the beginning of the rock clusters. Note that the trout in the deep part of the pool drop downstream and the fish in the runs move up. This usually happens at twilight and early in the morning. Quite often when a light hatch of flies is on the water the action will not be at the head of the pool but here at the tail. Also, the insect action brings the minnows up to feed, and big trout from the deep central part of the pool will drop down to chase them.

Work this area well, not by wading into it but by fishing from the side.

Fishing the Film

About the time that the water in your trout stream warms to fifty degrees there is a lot of action going on continually, all day and all night. Insects from the trees and banks are flying around and many are blown into the stream and some even crawl in. Aquatic insects—mayflies, caddis, stones and a host of others—also are active. Some are continuing to grow to the point when they will hatch, some are hatching, and some have hatched—all adding to the total of food choices available to the trout.

The water surface—that thin line between the air and the water itself—is a magical kind of area that attracts objects and insects that stick in the surface film. When the mayfly nymphs are hatching for example, they drift up from the bottom over a distance of miles and finally become stuck in the film, at which time they break open their nymphal shucks, hatch, and emerge to float on the surface for a while before finally taking off to shed their dun skin. (They return within twenty-four hours as adults or spin-

ners to lay their eggs to start the next cycle.) Caddis flies usually pop up from the bottom of the stream, bouyed by an air sac that surrounds their body until they hatch on the surface. . . .

These insects float in the film for miles, and it is in the film that the trout look for their dinner.

The floater should ride *in* the film, not over it. Most of our modern high-riding dry flies hardly dent the surface film, and it is quite possible—with all the real insects situated in the film itself— that the high-riding dries are harder for the trout to see. Tradition has taught us that the dry fly should float high and dry so we can see it there in the foam, bubbles, and shiny spots of water. And indeed this is good for us since it helps us to know what's happening. But what if the trout can't get a good look at our fly unless the fly breaks the film and is visible from below?

The old English fly-tyers generally used softer hackle than we

Americans do. Maybe they realized the need for the body of their flies to penetrate the surface film!

When the film is broken by rushes of water behind rocks and snags, and also by falls and white-water rapids, the dappled wet flies come into their own. The cast is made generally up and across the current. The rod is held high and the flies are allowed both to rest on the surface and sink below. In working them over a good run, rollcast a mend upstream above the rock or run you are interested in, let the flies drift down under the surface for a spell, draw them back toward you in a short series of jerks, and when the flies have drifted about ten feet downstream recast upstream and repeat the process. I have performed this routine many times and been about to give up when the action finally enticed a trout from way down deep to come up to investigate.

Another good trick in this type of water is to employ a dry fly on a tippet above the sunken fly. The dry fly will act as a bobber when a trout hits the wet one on the leader below. Quite often when fishing this way you'll experience light hits, and the dropper dry will tell you what's going on. Also it's quite possible a trout will actually jump for the dry fly instead of the wet.

It's unorthodox—and it catches fish!

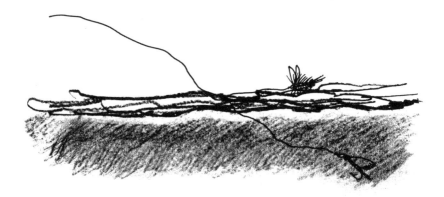

For many years I invested in fine web-free hackle that made my flies ride like puff balls on the water. I'd fish them even during a hatch and wonder why the trout didn't devour them immediately. Many members of the dry-fly fraternity cast and cast with little reward and wonder what is wrong. When Swisher-Richards came out with their hackle-less fly it was a great success. Why? One reason that Swisher-Richards suggest, and many of us support, is that the body of the hackle-less fly cuts the film and offers more visibility to the trout.

Look closely at a caddis fly that has just hatched and is resting on the water. Its wings are slanted back over its body and the body is at least half submerged. Look at the mayfly just hatched. Its body is resting on the water also. Look at the natural land-bred moths, butterflies, spiders, bugs—they are caught right in the film and are quite visible from below.

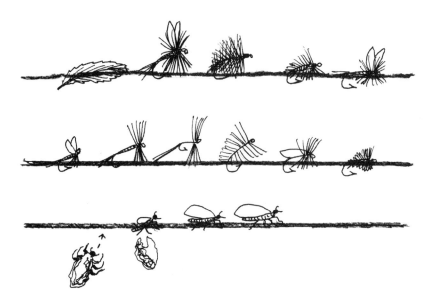

I'm not suggesting we throw away all our stiff-hackle flies and use only soggy ones. What I'm suggesting throughout this book is that we become disentangled from theories set forth by traditionalist angling scribes as arbitrary paths for us to follow.

Let's look at several situations and examine them with regard to fly choice and presentation.

First, let's look at a stretch of water that is flowing rather fast —but smoothly. It's not a pool, nor is it the broken white water found between pools. There are individual runs and turns in the current that are determined by the contour of the bottom well up-stream. These current lines carry the drifting insects and leaves and blow-in material that have collected way above and gradually been added to as the stream flows down. Wade out right now and submerge your net in one of the current flows. You'll collect all kinds of bark, branches, twigs, leaves, and insects. And you'll collect them from the surface, not from down deep. Some will be land-breds. Some will be aquatics, especially if a hatch has been in progress.

This is the food lane, the spot to fish with your dry fly. Since there is no action right now, use a fly that will settle into the film yet remain visible to you.

Choice of fly material, remember, has a great effect on just how the fly will sit on the water. A Quill body that is thin, smooth, and on stiff long hackles will hardly touch the water. But the fur body of the Cahill for example, or the peacock hurl of the Coach-man, will cut the film and get part of your fly submerged so the fish can see it.

Take up a position above a specific stretch and cast your flies over and above the run. Don't worry about keeping them afloat. Cast, let them drift, and when they are about to swing around below you, throw extra loops of line to extend the drift and slow down the curving course until the flies are lying in the water straight below your position. Now rollcast a pickup and dapple the flies back into the current in an upstream direction until they are almost opposite you. Then let them drift down again.

Much too often anglers will merely make vague casts to this type of water and not really work it thoroughly.

I've found that trout that are not actually on the feed during a rise will sometimes wait for several drifts of my flies before they decide to take. Usually we are in too much of a hurry to cover the water, and at just about the time a trout becomes interested we move on to what we think are greener pastures.

These subtle runs that carry the constant stream of food over the trout should be worked hard. These stretches are often over-looked by anglers who prefer to fish the pools, but the surface-film area in the runs is a hot spot, so work it well.

The food lanes and film accumulation of drifting insects be-comes even more enticing to the trout in the slower water—not glassy yet, but much slower and easier flowing. Again, the currents are dictated by underwater contours, so when you see a large disturbance in this quiet water, look upstream a couple of yards and you'll probably see a boulder or a sudden rise of gravel. That's where the trout could be resting, so instead of casting your flies to the breaks in the current, work well above them. One of the points I want to stress in this book is that you should always, always concentrate on a given spot and direct your presentation accordingly. So, now you will fish for an unseen trout over an unseen cluster of boulders. Cast up and across so that your flies will drift right over the area. Use a brace of wets, a dry fly, or even a couple of nymphs. It doesn't much matter for you are hunting at this point.

Learn to read this kind of water and seek out the spots where the trout are, not where the water is the most active.

I usually leave the flat stretches until the shadows begin to lengthen, since the trout will be asleep or certainly not bent on exposing themselves unless a great amount of food is being drifted over them in the film. Again, fish will not be found on the bare bottom, but will hide alongside rocks and boulders or along ledges of gravel and along overhangs. When the light is right you can spot them, but more often than not they will not be seen. You have to have faith that they are there and plan your moves accordingly. The wet fly technique is down and across holding the rod high, skittering the flies so that they break the surface film. This is quite the opposite of the dry-fly fisherman's drag-free, delicate fishing, but it works. If you want, try the dry fly first.

One of the best times to fish the film is mid-season, but get up early. The insects that have been either hatching, as in the case of stone flies and all of the night creatures such as moths, millers, and other crawly things, will be drifting downstream. They might possibly have reached the water miles above while it was still dark. The first early-morning breezes cut them loose from their perches in the trees and brush along the bank of the stream.

The light is still dull and the trout have not yet searched out their pet hiding places for the bright light of day to come. If the morning is overcast, so much the better, you'll likely have more time at it.

I like to fish two small wet flies and perhaps a dropper dry fly on a ten-foot leader in this situation. I go armed with my longest rod, a nine-footer. Usually it is not necessary to wade out into the stream unless there is a pet run I want to cover that cannot be reached from the bank.

Cast in the old-fashioned way—across—and let the flies drift. Skitter them back up again or even mend the entire cast upstream for a fresh try at the run. Work downstream too, but let your cast drift well below you and then let it swing slowly to the stream edge. But most important, spot those feed lanes that are loaded with goodies that the trout like.

Fly pattern is not important here, just cast and recast and work these areas well. If the section you are fishing is semi-broken water you can spend a good deal of time on it without the danger of putting any fish down. Work the slower glassy stretches a bit more carefully, allowing a long drift before recasting.

After an all-night gentle rain is another time to be out on the stream. Even if the rain has occurred in the daytime, get out there immediately after it. That rain has drenched a lot of insects and they will be floating right on the film. There is something about a rain that excites trout and usually they feed avidly once the sun begins to break through and will stay at it until the stream becomes too bright.

The most obvious time to fish the feed lanes and work the film is during a hatch. The flies stick in the film to cast their nymphal shuck and are fair game to the marauders from below. Dry flies are your first choice during the hatch, or, again, use my pet ruse, the dry fly on the tippet as a bobber and a wet fly on the end. Keep the rod high, with only the leader in the water.

Quite often a hatch of mayflies will occur way upstream from you while nothing is hatching in the water in which you are fishing. From literally out of nowhere they will descend, riding like little sailboats right in the feed lanes and in the film. Since there is no hatch coming off right where you are, the trout will take some time to see them. When finally this happens, you'll have action. Dry flies again for sure this time and make your casts as gentle as possible. Avoid drag. These flies are not active on the surface, they are just going for a ride.

Don't neglect the twilight, especially in mid-season when the adult mayflies—spinners—will be returning as the temperature drops and the light darkens. Mating and dancing over the water in

profusion, some of them—particularly the females with their loaded egg sacs—will be first call on the trout's menu. Dry flies again and spent-wing patterns in particular.

When the trout decide it's time really to pay attention to what's going on in that film, they will rise from the bottom and hang lazily in the current, their noses pointed up and their bodies at a slight angle. You'll likely not find them doing this in the fast water, so look for them in the slower stretches, particularly at the tails of pools . . . or even in the back waters of big pools where ordinarily you would not cast. The drifting film sometimes circles back into these backwaters and the trout know it.

Fish the film thoroughly. Sure, in another section of the book I suggest you sink your flies. But that's another technique for another specific situation. I've found that both the film and the very bottom are the most potent areas to fish. Seldom have I taken trout from the midwater.

When I fish the film, as I do most of the time except perhaps in the early spring, I am not as concerned with pattern as I am with seeing to it that my flies drift as naturally as possible. I have never seen a specific pattern outfish all others. Fishing three flies to the leader will prove this, and for exercise and knowledge I've fished this way many times. I cannot remember when out of three wet— or dry—flies on the leader, one specific pattern was hit ALL THE TIME.

Another subject closely related to fishing the film is midge fishing, and when I think about it my temper begins to rise. I've tied a lot of size-22 flies in my time and spent hours on the water fishing them on gossomer leaders. And sure, I've caught some trout on them. But it's impossible to say that those tiny flies were the ONLY flies the trout would've gone for.

I'll throw one at you now that will be a surprise. It is the four-winged fly. Yes that's right, a four-winged dry fly with or without hackle. Now here's a fly that really cuts the film. Thinking that some of the insects just might get tumbled enough to have their wings pointing downward on the surface, I tied the four-wing fly one night, just for kicks. It isn't easy to tie. You tie in the bottom wings first, slightly behind where you'll place the legitimate up-wings. Use hackle if you like, though the fly floats just as well on the four wings, two of which are bound to puncture the surface film.

Looked at from below they are sure "buggy looking."

But don't tell anyone I told you of this gimmick . . . it works!

Big Fly—Big Trout

. . . an old saying among the old guard who were brought up on wet flies and streamers and bucktails. Most of these anglers were big-fish-happy and would go after only the biggies, much preferring to risk returning home fishless.

I learned to use big flies for trout while studying under Ed Sens on the Neversink in the Catskills. He took me night fishing at about ten o'clock. He armed me with a size-8 stone fly imitation that was a fluffy and scraggly concoction of wings, rabbit fur, and soft hackles. He dipped it in dry fly dope and told me to cast it out and across the stream, play out the slack, and prepare for a rise.

A rise I got—a good solid one, and one of the biggest trout of my life was on the other end.

Night fishing with the big flies became a passion, but strangely enough, during the day I'd revert back to my small flies, even to the 20s and 22s.

It was only later, after walking along a stream one day and seeing the discarded stonefly nymph cases, that it dawned on me that with the abundance of big stone flies, and big caddis for that matter, found in most eastern streams and virtually all western waters, I should use a big fly if I really wanted to connect with something to photograph.

I'm a slow learner but once on the track I'll not give up. I concocted several abominations that would never sell or even impress a drunk and went forth in search of predator trout.

The first day out was a bright one just ahead of the green drake hatch on the Au Sable in upper New York State. Hatches of giant stone flies appear on this water just before the fabulous green drake hatch that drives dry fly fishermen wild for about two weeks out of each year.

Sure enough, the discarded shucks of the hatched stoneflies were all along the shoreline. It seems they come ashore onto a rock at night, split open their shuck, and take off into the air.

Now bright sunlight and clear water would hardly seem the ideal conditions under which to work monstrous flies on the surface as dries, or even as sunken wets . . . but something in my perverse nature revolted against all the theory, so I went forth to war.

First I worked the big wets in a weighted-nymph pattern. Armed with my old nine-foot rod and a leader tapered to 3-X I tied on two of my special patterns, took up a position above the head of a pool, cast the flies right where the white water stopped, fed out the slack to let them sink, and on almost every cast I got a bump. Finally a real taker swallowed the hook well below the base of his tongue. After landing two more (the smallest of these 15 inches), I retired to a bar, where I knew I'd find some of the gang, to brag.

Big fly, big trout. . . .

I'll also never forget fishing on the Housatonic River in Connecticut and seeing a sight I could hardly believe. I had spent the morning fishing some of my entomologically perfect size-16 nymphal imitations to no avail when I finally reached one of the roadside parks. There were several people there, and a couple of kids were fishing from the edge of the stream.

While my flies were drifting casually down in front of me, I saw one of the youngsters' rods break into an arc. He let out a howl that was echoed in the hills and I saw the splashing of water in front of him. Instantly the other kids gathered around him as he valiantly fought the fish—a smallmouth bass I figured (since it was making quite a fuss)—and finally, amid yells and yanks, the fish was unceremoniously flopped up on the bank and pounced on by eager hands.

I decided to come ashore to offer my congratulations (and incidentally to find out what had caused that fish to hit). The catch turned out to be a fine plump brown about a foot long (a nice fish in that river, believe me), and I asked the usual question, almost certain he would answer back "worm."

Instead, he produced for my examination what to this day still shocks me, even when I tie one for myself.

It was a panfish bug. Green body, six elastic legs. Size-10 hook. In comparison with conventional dry flies it was a monster.

He couldn't wait to cast it out again, and so help me God, he took a second and a third trout right there on three casts.

Now any expert who has fished the Housatonic and has bought his flies from Jim Deren's Anglers Roost Tackle Store knows that the trout in that river are sophisticated, smart, crafty, shy, and feed only on flies tied by published authors. In all the years I've fished that water I have never taken more than one or two in a morning—or perhaps three in an evening . . . but this youngster! No one had told him that panfish flies are not designed to take trout! No one had told him the trout were sophisticated!

It was a long time before that event started to simmer down in my memory.

Big fly, big trout.

It's a commonsense approach to fishing and one that should be encouraged.

Far be it from me to tell you to scrap all your fancy creations and those of the famed experts and go buy panfish flies. All I'm saying is that we should keep our eyes open to possibilities beyond our restricting beliefs, traditions, and personal biases.

More often than not the big fly need not be fished dead-drift in the current but rather can be activated on the surface—fished like an escaping form of life. You can fish the dry fly like a bass bug. In fact I've tied small bass bugs for some years now and I use them successfully in the bright light of day in clear water when you would think only a small fly would be taken.

Grasshoppers too are prime trout food, especially in the country, where the streams flow through the fields and open land where these insects abound.

Even if they are not found in profusion near your pet stream, grasshoppers are still a good bet.

This was brought home to me one time on the Esopus. An angler from England was visiting with a friend of mine and we had

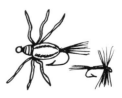

the old gent on the stream for several days, for we were proud of our Catskill rivers and eager for him to tie into a really good fish to talk about when he returned to England.

Four days had gone by and all he had taken on his British dries were some limit-size browns of the hatchery variety. While he had seen some really big fish rise he just hadn't connected.

Then came his last afternoon—our last chance to come up with something spectacular. My friend Joe made a suggestion that was a shocker but we all agreed to give it a try. Joe and several of us went out to the nearby field and caught grasshoppers, no easy task in the middle of a hot day. Then Joe took the mason jar filled with them and walked up to the bridge above the pool where the Englishman was fishing. One by one Joe dropped the hoppers into the river and we could see them drifting downstream through the fast water just above where our guest was casting.

As the hoppers began to drift directly above him we saw a splashing rise near his fly and then another, and another. He saw that the trout were rising and cast furiously to them. All of a sudden we saw his rod spring into a circle and his line tighten down to a great splash. He was fast to a good fish. Netting it properly he held it high for all of us to see and I went down to the stream edge to take it from him so he could return to the river. He did so and those trout rose as long as the hoppers lasted and enabled our friend to creel two more big trout.

Big nymph, big trout also applies, particularly in the early season when the water is roily and visibility is not too good even for sharp-eyed trout. Sink those big stonefly imitations. Use three at a time if you can stand to be so unorthodox. Sink them deep and let them bounce around in the currents. Fish the fast water too, letting them swing in an arc below you and gradually inching them in by coiling the line in your hand on the intake. Rollcast them right back over the same water you've just fished.

Even though I've had great success for years with big flies, I've always considered them a last resort. Why, I don't know, unless all my theories have gotten in the way of common sense.

Many's the time I've lost patience, tied on a big fanwing dry, and slapped it down unceremoniously on a stretch my fellow scribes describe as dry-fly water.

More often than not the decision has led to success, even if it contradicts all the matching-the-hatch dogma we "experts" generally go by.

Over the years I have known a few anglers who are true specialists—not purists, but specialists—who fish exclusively for big trout and big trout only. I call them trout hunters—big game specialists—and a lot can be learned from them.

Elsewhere in this book I write about an expert minnow fisherman and how he can rake 'em in. But Nick is also a bucktail angler, and he likes to fish these big flies as much as he does live minnows. He says the bucktail, properly fished, can be even more deadly than the minnow.

I've watched Nick work some of the big pools in our Catskill streams and at one time we fished several of the streams in Montana together.

Nick hunts his trout in several ways, using bucktails exclusively. His flies are tied on monstrous hooks, 6's mostly, medium shank and heavy. When he can't get the right ones he uses salt-water hooks that can really sink a fly down deep. His flies are short and stocky, full, and are mounted on silver-and-gold bodies. The wings contain a generous amount of polar bear fur.

He uses two basic approaches.

One might be called the standard across-and-down drift-and-retrieve. He'll cast across and slightly downstream, bringing his fly (or flies) down about twenty-five feet above a midstream rock or some obvious break in the current. Then, feeding out line, he allows the fly to sink (but *not* dead drift—he always has control of the fly and can feel it, he says, all the time).

"No sense in allowing that fly to be so free you can't feel it in the current. If a fish hits it you'll never know it."

He times the action so the fly will begin to circle around from the effect of the current at just the right spot: just ahead of the break in the current. He knows from years of experience that this is where the big trout lie.

When the fly is just beginning to swing he gives it a mighty jerk, snapping it up from the bottom and breaking the surface. He skitters that fly from a high-held rod, straight upstream from the spot, and then immediately drops it down again, throwing slack line to let it sink down.

He repeats this process several times.

"Those big trout don't usually hit on the first, second, or

even third time I do this. They take a little teasing, and I give it to them.''

He uses this technique too when fishing above a white-water break, casting his flies into the white water and letting them sink fast right at the edge of the break. He keeps a tight line all the time, but at the same time throws extra line and raises his rod so his flies act naturally.

I asked him about light hits.

''Sure I get a lot of light hits, but those are usually from smaller trout. When the big ones strike they mean business.''

Nick concentrates only on the hottest spots.

''It may be an arbitrary decision, but I've found that you can waste a lot of time on water where the big fish just don't hang out. Fish the water immediately beneath the white water at the head of a pool. That's just common sense. But don't show yourself. Fish it from way above or if you can't do that from as far away to the side as possible. Approach the area very slowly. Don't just walk up to the stream edge and cast. The smaller trout might put up with it, but the big ones are easily spooked and will descend into the deeper water and thus be harder to entice.

''Work the edges of shelving riffles, beginning from well above them and staying out of sight as much as possible. Remember, you are hunting, not just casting. The deep holes are harder to fish. If you wade to them you have to do it carefully and very slowly and if any other fishermen have been in the water nearby forget the spot and move away to untouched water.

''Don't neglect the tails of the pools at twilight and even after dark. The big fish like to slip downstream into the shallows and root out minnows. That's the time you'll connect, but again, you have to stalk them.''

I know another angler who fishes all over the world using the very unorthodox method of skittering his big heavy flies right across the surface!

''I scare the hell out of the little trout, but the big ones love it and those are the ones I'm after.''

I've seen him do this and expected that no trout would ever rise in that water again. Strangely enough one, a big one would often come up and grab his fly and the battle would be on.

''I learned this trick in Europe fishing for Atlantic salmon,'' he told me. ''Over there they do this quite a bit to shake the big ones into action. Once they get them excited, they strike."

Jim Deren, possibly the most famous trout fisherman in the East, and Larry Koller are two of the best poachin' anglers I have ever known. Larry used to know the lower Neversink well—before the present reservoirs were built—and one time when I was making a movie of him, he showed his prowess at taking big trout from that water. A small trout looks even smaller to the camera, and I needed trout at least fifteen inches or better really to show him off.

Larry tied a most unusual bucktail. Actually it was a bucktail-streamer, tied with two streamer feathers and sided with a few wisps of bucktail and polar bear. He'd dredge the bottom of those very rocky and pockety waters and usually before long would have a good trout hooked.

Deren used a big heavy nymph for his trout hunting.

"If you want big trout, fish that big nymph like a worm. You don't have to cast a country mile. Just plop 'em in and drift 'em down," he'd tell me.

Another trout hunter asked me one day if I had ever examined the stomach of a really big trout.

"You'll find they feed almost exclusively on minnows and small trout. I've taken many with six- and seven-inch trout in their bellies. They are the monsters of the stream, and grow that big because most anglers don't know how to fish for them—or don't even figure that trout that big live in the stream!"

Big-trout hunting requires a big, strong, powerful rod with a stiff tip. Most of the time the rod is held high in order to take up the slack you produce with even a modest cast. *Big rod* doesn't mean *long cast*. It means control of the line once it's in the water, whether you feed your line out right from where you're standing or make a short cast.

It could be argued that to fish for big trout long casts would be necessary so as not to scare the monsters down. In all but the most open water however, those trout are down deep and hiding. They're not dallying about in the midstream currents or snooping up at drifting flies except at night. . . .

Long casts are fun to see, but they make it impossible to control the line and direct the fly properly. Make your casts short and to the point, and handle your line like a hunter. Keep in touch with your fly *at all times*.

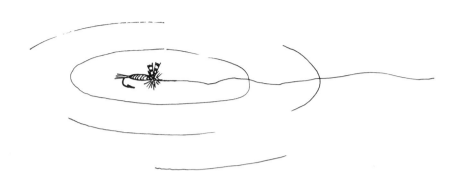

Thoughts On the Dry Fly

First of all, the dry fly doesn't have to be dry.

Most anglers will fish their dries on water where the fly will float—and a lot of fish are missed this way. The fast water, where your dry fly won't float for more than a few seconds, can be a prime spot. Fish those dry flies wet and you'll get hits. An overcast mid-season day when there have already been some hatches is a fine time to go after the faster stretches with your dries.

You can cast upstream either directly or at a slight angle, shooting for the basic currents that would most likely be carrying dead-drift flies down from the waters above.

Don't worry about your fly floating. No natural fly will float in such fast water, and neither should yours. You make the cast, allow the fly to drift until it is pulled under by the currents, retrieve by rollcasting forward, and drop the fly right back into the same run. Do this again and again, gradually working your way down, or across.

This is the kind of water where big trout will hang out on a bright day. The only other place they can rest the hot sunlight out is on the very bottom of the deep pools, under the very lips of falls, or under clusters of big boulders.

Fast water and boulder-broken stretches harbor big trout, and even though they are not on the feed in this position, they are alert to what's happening on the surface.

The strike to the dry fly under these conditions will be decisive. Since they don't have time to look the fly over they'll hit hard and you'll likely find they've taken the fly deep in the throat.

So don't pass up that fast water when you're fishing dry.

It's a gold mine.

What about the slower, glassy stretches?

Too often we just wander along casting our dries upstream and hoping for something to happen.

There are trout under that surface . . . but how do you get them to strike?

If nothing's rising, you might try fishing the film, as I discuss in another chapter—sinking that dry fly a little bit so the fish can see it better.

Another trick on slow water calls for the use of two flies. Rig your dry-fly leader with an extra tippet about six inches long and tie it in about a foot from the end. Use a different pattern the same size as your first. I bet you'll fish for a long time before you see a dry-fly fisherman using more than one fly on his leader, but just because he doesn't do it doesn't mean you shouldn't.

Still another trick, when you're fishing over gently moving water, is to cast across-stream rather than straight up. When the fly lights, allow it to drift a couple of feet and then, using a roll-cast pickup, drop it back in the same position again—and again. This is a particularly good way to coax a trout out from under an undercut bank.

If you can, target your fly so it actually bumps the grass and bounces back into the water. Allow it to drift a few feet and recast the same way.

There's a trout in under that bank.

When you're working a stretch of water that's glassy, the perfect treatment is the drag-free drift of traditional fame.

However, if you try this cast and it doesn't produce, jiggle that fly and don't worry about making a fuss. Experiment, for you've got nothing to lose.

I remember a day I and my good friend the late Mark Kerridge were fishing the Metolius in Oregon. It was one of those glorious Oregon days with puffy clouds that obscured the sun once in a while, and a cool breeze gently blowing downstream. We had fished apart for some time with Mark in the lead. We were casting dry flies—small ginger quills (usually a good fly on that stream in mid-season). But neither of us had had a tumble.

Finally Mark called me up to him and we decided to try the old ruse of creating a hatch.

We began casting to a center current that was a bit ruffled by some underwater rocks. As soon as his fly had drifted down about two feet from where it had landed, I placed mine just above it. We let the flies drift about five feet and then recast the same way. After about four tries he got a tumble from a trout and the hit was solid. I kept casting to the same spot as he allowed the fish to fight and tumble downstream out of the way. Shortly I was into a small rainbow and it was all we could do to keep from tangling.

Both Mark and I are skeptics. So we waded upstream about fifty feet to another current break and repeated the performance.

While we were casting, another angler was seen on the bank, evidently watching us.

"Saw you guys connect down below. What are you casting—what pattern?" he asked.

"Ginger quill," Mark responded. "Come join us."

We explained we had fished for an hour or so without any rises but were employing the old trick of creating a hatch and lined him up with us. Soon three dry flies were being cast to a point just ahead of the very slight break in the current and then drifting down, about two feet apart.

Mark was again the first to connect with the whopping rise of a good-sized rainbow, but it must have been hooked lightly and it got away. We continued to cast in this fashion and soon the newcomer had a busting rise and his fly snapped off because he struck too soundly. I was next in line for action and just as I was about to pick up my fly for the recast, a trout struck and bit off the fly.

"That's the most action I've seen in two days," the newcomer announced.

We marched upstream to a fresh stretch where we had seven strikes—and three hooked fish.

There had been no sign of a hatch on the water. There were no drifting flies, and an examination of the film showed that nothing was drifting down, not even any land-bred insects!

The Forgotten Wet Fly

It's unfortunate the anglers of today have missed the period of those colorful and numberless wet flies that were concocted over a hundred years ago in England and later in the U.S. Those who have a copy of Ray Bergman's TROUT can relish looking at the countless plates of colorful wet-fly patterns tied by Dr. Burke. Many of these patterns called for feathers and skill not generally available today.

Whether it might be advisable to use these patterns instead of the more contemporary drab patterns designed as insect imitations is a moot point. It seems that almost any combination of color and shape will take trout at some time or other, and certainly conventional wet-fly fishing in the old style—two or three flies to the leader—is not a bad way to creel enough trout for supper.

Most of us old-timers can remember using the old system with great success—until we became specialists in the exact-imitation school of fly-tying and gradually allowed the old conventional wets to go by the boards.

During my many years of fly-tying experimentation, especially with nymphs, I've gotten my comeuppance more than once from anglers using the old wet patterns and techniques.

One such time was on the Neversink, when I was deep into fly-tying experimentation with Ed Sens, who as far as I'm concerned tied the best nymphs I've ever seen. Well, his father pooh-poohed Ed's ventures into the exact-imitation school, and the old man was fishing with us one night, using the same flies he'd been fishing with all season long. I think he had a brown hackle, a lead-wing coachman, and a battered and fish-gnawed silver doctor on his heavy-snelled leader.

To put it mildly, Ed and I with our scrupulously tied nymphs and dainty leader technique could not compete with the man with the three old wets. He merely rolled them out over the water, raised his rod tip, and skittered them over the surface of the runs. Within ten minutes he had five strikes and landed three trout 15 inches or better.

We took none that evening.

Another time was on the Allagash River in Maine, after the guide and I had gone ashore from our canoe to set up camp for the evening. He assembled his rod, with three wet flies dangling from heavy-snelled leaders, and placed the rod in the stern of the canoe, which was pointing out into the current. He fed the flies out by hand from the reel and came ashore.

Just about the time our fire was blazing I noticed the rod vibrating wildly and went to investigate. When I lifted it up there were TWO fat brook trout thumping away—our first trout of the day. Thinking that the twilight was the magic I immediately got my rod and flailed the water with my flies—but all I caught were chubs.

Now I do not suggest we throw away all the books of fame and merit that have come down the pike these last forty years. I do not mean we stick on a heavy-snelled leader with two droppers and forget all we've learned in our scientific experiments. But I do say we should not rule out the simple approach, especially if our creel is light.

Recently I visited an uncle of mine now in his eighties. He can still cast a fly and when we ventured down to the stream he was carrying a whippy old bamboo rod with a line at least forty years old and believe it or not a gut leader with two snells and a tippet fly. As we approached the stream he soaked the leader in his mouth and in a few minutes it was limp enough to cast. I watched him take four trout—nice ones—fishing from the bank rollcasting not over twenty feet of line. Author of several books on the involved techniques of trouting I stood there watching a dear old man who hadn't read any of them show me up for good.

I think we've been guided by too many experts who have invented new and more interesting—but not necessarily more potent —ways to take trout. We've been taught that trout are leader-shy, that they've become more sophisticated, that the simple old ways are no longer valid on the trout stream.

The therapy for this generation of fly fishermen seems to consist of very complicated theories and very specific types of equipment . . . new fly patterns and a degree in entomology. . . .

Maybe trouting is beginning to suffer from over-intellectualism!

Once when no one was looking I tied up some heavy nylon leaders tapered to about 3X and including two tippets. I went to my fly tying bench, made up a brown hackle, a leadwing coachman, and a light Cahill, and took off for the Esopus, another fine Catskill stream that can boast 20-inch rainbows and bigger browns all season long. I went forth with my old style rig and began casting, not from a picture pose in midstream but from the shore. It wasn't long before I connected with a keeper and then a bigger one and yet a still bigger trout. I released all of them, figuring I'd keep the last one or two for tomorrow's breakfast. It occurred to me that I'd suddenly gained a lot of confidence out of nowhere. How did I know I was going to catch any more?

Somehow I just knew. And I did catch more. I caught several more by that very simple method and ate them the next morning for breakfast.

Cast them out into a run of current. No need to wade. Just

stand there on the bank and rollcast them out. Keep your rod high and let the leader skitter those flies across the water and—*whammo*!

Let the water settle down a little or walk downstream to a fresh spot and repeat the cast. . . .

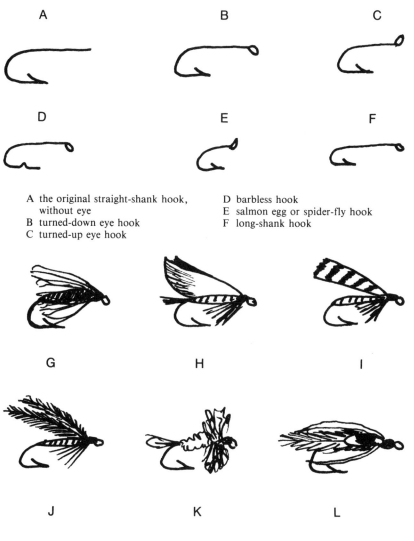

A the original straight-shank hook, without eye
B turned-down eye hook
C turned-up eye hook
D barbless hook
E salmon egg or spider-fly hook
F long-shank hook

G hair fly with thick body
H duckwing wet-fly
I flank-feather section-winged wet fly
J hackle-wing wet fly
K hair fly (similar to the dry style)
L salmon-type wet fly with golden pheasant top and bottom

Wet fly hooks and wet flies

The wet fly—along with its counterpart the dry—started in England, the birthplace of fly fishing. Most of the standard patterns that still exist today were designed by British gentlemen who were the beginning artistic fly tiers. A hundred years ago the wet fly and dry also became the sportsman's flies in America, as fly tyers copied the English patterns and also devised patterns of their own. While the dry fly developed a clique of snobs who regarded the wet fly as a chuck-and-chance-it form of unartistic angling, the wet fly consistently caught fish.

In those early days gut leaders were the only ones available. They had to be moistened before use and required special care so they would not become brittle. The dry fly was fished as a single fly but the wet fly could be used three to a leader by tying a leader with a stepped-down taper with loops at each taper joint. The wet fly was tied on an eyeless hook with the leader tied directly to the hook shank under the body dressing. A loop at the top of the leader was attached to the main leader loop. If the leader was not properly soaked and softened it would break off at the fly's head, so great care was taken to assure resiliency in the leader. In a later version (the eyed-fly-hook) the leader was either tied in as before but through the eye, or the eyed fly was tied with a turle knot directly to the leader end. This offered the possibility of frequent pattern change.

The leaders were at first seldom more than five feet in length, and later were designed to seven feet, just short of the rod length, since the loops could not be drawn down through the rod guides.

The leaders were fished on level lines, as tapered lines were yet to come on the scene, and thus casting distance was limited to twenty to thirty feet at the most. As a result the angler would roll-cast his wet flies from the bank and work all the stream edges upstream and down.

It's amazing how many trout were taken from the stream edges and snags. Yet today you will seldom see anglers working the stream edges. They wade up the middle and concentrate on the midstream rocks and currents . . . and they miss some good bets.

With the demise of the old wet fly a great fishing style went by the boards. Just for fun, when no one is looking turn back the clock a few years and dapple and skitter some wet flies over the runs you can reach with a thirty-foot cast. Work the shoreline snags and the undercuts. Don't wade.

Just for tradition's sake tie a white wing coachman on top, a march brown or a dark Cahill in the middle, and a black gnat on the end. Or try a parmachene Belle on top, a brown hackle in the middle, and a silver doctor on the end. If you can't find these patterns at the store, look 'em up in an old book and tie 'em yourself.

And while you're at it fish two streamers or bucktails on that same leader once in a while, letting them sink in the current out there beside you and tricking them in and around in a downstream swing . . . or tie a wet fly on the dropper and a small bucktail on the end. . . .

It's generally agreed that you've got to activate your wet flies in order to make them attractive to the trout. But what do you do when your wets are down deep where you can't see them or feel very well what they're doing?

Well, of course you activate them with line and rod-tip action as usual. But is the action getting to the flies? And if so, what effect is it producing?

I could write you paragraphs of theory here, which would mainly represent my and other's guesses about what's going on down there with your fly . . . but why not experiment and see for yourself? Tie on an oversized white-winged fly and let it go way deep and do a little experimenting. Twitch your rod tip and gather in some line and watch to see what, if any, the action really is. Chances are you'll discover you have to give your rig more action than you thought.

This kind of experimentation (instead of depending on the books) is rare. It's rare because fishermen are lazy, and because they can't bring themselves to give up fishing for half an hour to do a little stream-based research. All they can think about is how many fish they're going to catch.

If they'd just give up a little of their fishing time and spend it experimenting, their chances for action—and for their dream-lunker—would be doubled.

And when you get into the habit of devoting a little time now and then to experimentation—experimentation with a specific problem in mind—you find after a while that it becomes almost as rewarding and fun as fishing!

Now let's get out on the water again and get to work.

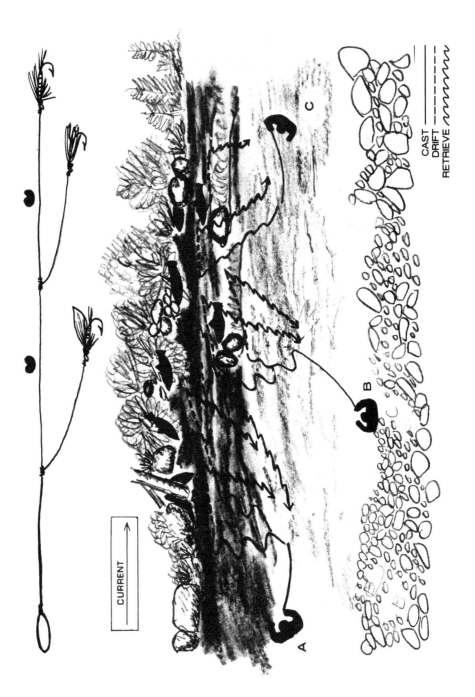

CURRENT

CAST
DRIFT ——————
RETRIEVE ~~~~~~~

A

B

C

Flowing as it does along beside—and in under— an enticing overhang, this is a hard stretch to fish. The idea is to get your flies in as close as possible, even if it means risking getting hung up. Don't worry about drag, and forget about trying to activate your flies. Just get them in under there where the trout are waiting.

From A, throw a cast on a slack line right to the stream edge, raising your rod tip immediately to keep your line out of the water as much as possible and also to enable you to guide your leader as your flies drift downstream. Don't try for too long a run. Rollcast-pickup your flies and drop them again, this time a bit further downstream than before, throwing a bit of slack for them to absorb on the drift. Work your retrieves in short jerks.

From B, work those two rocks directly across-stream from you first. Put your flies on the near side of the rocks and retrieve with a twitch . . . then above, and below, and on the far side too if you can get to it. From C, work the large submerged rock as shown . . . then move your casts in closer.

In all cases and positions work your casts closer and closer in toward the bank until you are getting right to the edge of the overhang. If you can, get in under the overhang. That's where the big ones are.

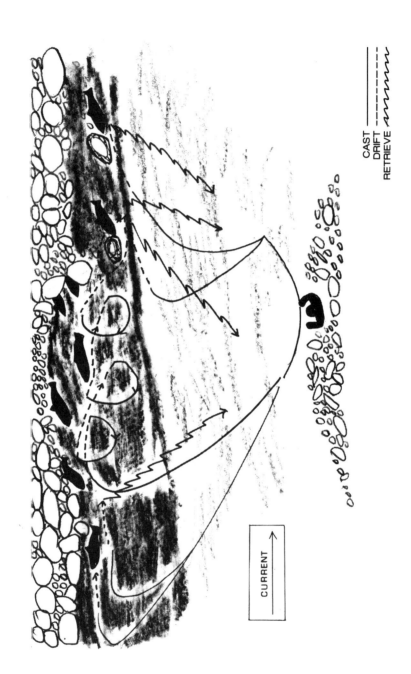

CURRENT

CAST ————
DRIFT ------
RETRIEVE ~~~~~~

Your position overlooks the far bank with its deep current. Stay as far away as possible so as not to drive back any trout that might be lying out from the bank. If there are insects about, either land-breds or a drifting hatch coming down, the trout that normally lie in close to the edge will be out a bit from the shoreline, so move with caution and cast only when you mean business. Call your shots to a specific area and work it. Starting from the left, throw a loop of line well above the stretch and as soon as your flies begin to drift down throw another length of line to the same spot as before. Allow the drift to continue. Activate the flies on the return and work them right up almost to your rod tip.

On the second cast repeat the performance, but this time roll and mend upstream—just a smidgeon of line, just enough to pick the flies up in front of a trout and flip them back again. This is a great technique and may be repeated again and again over a particularly hot spot. Retrieve in jerks, pausing at the edge of the deep water for another drift.

The last cast is across and down. Activate those flies! Quite often merely by throwing those flies over there you activate a trout or two, and they just might venture out to look for a goodie.

Dry-fly casting requires a tight bow in order to work up power and speed for the forward delivery, especially if you're using a fast-action rod. When throwing your three wet flies however, things are vastly different—or should be. Try and slow down, remembering that those three flies on the end of your leader require a much slower cast, both forward and back. Moreover, your bow must be much wider. This requires a bit of subtle wrist and forearm action. Begin the backcast as usual but add just a touch of a second effort, and lift your forearm and turn your wrist up slightly. As the line goes back raise a bit more. On the drop-down keep the rod up—almost at the vertical—so that only your leader and flies are on the water.

You want to keep your casts short. Better to make a short, controllable cast and then get out more line, if you need it, by hand.

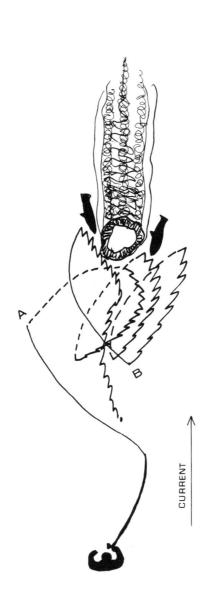

CURRENT

CAST ——————
DRIFT ————————
RETRIEVE ∿∿∿∿∿

Here's a routine to master for all your down-stream wet-fly fishing. Cast to A and allow the current to drag your flies across-stream. Pay out line as they drift to sink them a bit and when they reach the rock begin very quick and short jerks back upstream, guiding your line back over to your left. Make the drift again, paying out a bit more line to drop your flies down closer to the rock, and zig-zag them back up, again to your left. Repeat the drift, to the right, to point B, where you roll-cast and pick up to drop the flies down to the area just below the rock, zig-zagging the retrieve as before.

Be brave and work your flies over the rock, roll-ing them when necessary.

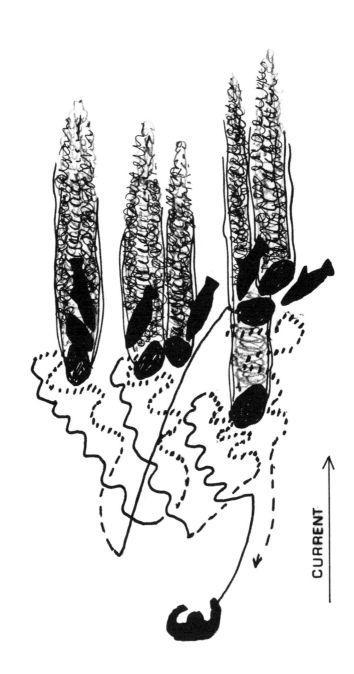

CURRENT

Skittering is a top tactic when working three wet flies and trying to bring action from a stream that seems to be, for all practical purposes, dead.

Take up a position above the cluster of rocks and drop your flies on a slack line. Let them sink and when they're where you want them raise your rod tip and pull back slightly to bring them to the surface. Diddle them across the water in short spurts, back and forth, rolling your line if need be. Keep that rod up and your line out of the water as much as possible.

When you get a strike when you're skittering like this, it's almost always a decisive take. You don't have to worry about reacting to set the hook.

The shelving riffle is perfect for skittering your wet flies or working them deep, depending where you ascertain the fish to be.

If the fish have come up to the edge of the riffle, take up a position that keeps you as far back from the shelf as possible and make your cast upstream. Let your flies drift a bit. Then, raising your rod tip skitter your flies right over the lip of the shelf . . . ; and when the cast is played out roll those flies back upstream and repeat.

Of course if the fish are down beyond the shelf in the deep water you have to go for them there, casting from a position further forward and making sure you get your flies down to the level of the fish.

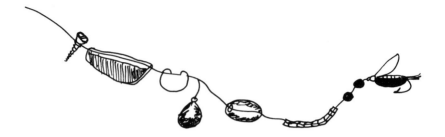

Sink That Fly!

Nick was an experienced and productive minnow fisherman that frequented many of the stretches of my home stream. I'd see him burst forth from the alders on a crisp spring day, place his can of minnows in the protected water at the stream edge, impale one of the minnows on a hook, swing his weighted leader out into the current, and wade into the water, gradually and slowly following the bait as it drifted downstream, wading not ten feet from shore and using not over twenty feet of line.

If I kept watching I'd see at least four big trout netted and creeled in less than a half hour. Then he'd come ashore, clean the fish, and drive back to town to begin his day at the local eatery.

I'd join him an hour or two later, bringing in my just-over-the-limit-sized browns for him to deep-fry and figuring that I had been a success that morning. I'd be tired from wading in over my hips, battling the cold spring current and flailing my newest nymph creations that were taken avidly by the chubs and by shiners. I liked Nick, but I had a high disregard for his adherance to minnow fishing. I was always trying to convert him to fishing with a fly, even if it was a weighted one.

Finally one morning he agreed to join me just for the fun of it, but he said the main reason he was able to catch those bigger trout was that he got his bait down to where the fish were—deep down, right on the bottom. He borrowed two of my big wet flies, tied them on his leader, and began fishing them the same way he did his live bait. And the results were almost the same. I think it took him longer to catch his morning limit of four fish, but he did it.

Meanwhile I was fishing the same patterns he was using, casting them out into the stream and looking good and catching nothing.

"Sink those flies, Ray, or you're wasting your time," he said as he lugged his heavy catch back to the restaurant.

I tried it and it worked. And since that time I've used his commonsense approach often, particularly in the early spring when there are no hatches on the water . . . and at times even in mid-season, when there is nothing going on that you can see in the form of feeding fish.

In the early-spring time of heavy water the trout will stay deep, resting behind big sunken boulders or along the shelves— anywhere that is out of the fastest currents. I guess they don't like to work harder than necessary just to stay in one place.

They are not actively on the feed, but in the springtime they're usually hungry constantly and will gobble up anything that drifts by them, be it a worm, a minnow, or nymphs and larvae dislodged by anglers wading the stream above.

Later in the season, when the water is low and the trout are not prone to hiding along the stream edges waiting for worms to be washed in by the rains and drains from the woods, they still remain deep simply because of the clear water and bright sunlight. Only a drifting cluster of nymphs about to hatch would bring them up, and even a hatch on the surface doesn't always make them ride high unless conditions are perfect. The deep-water pools and runs are where they stay. Even when feeding on caddis larvae, rooting around flashing their pretty sides and tails to the light, they hug the bottom most of the time. Very early in the morning, or late in the evening, some of the big ones will venture forth if

There are numerous ways to weight flies. Many tyers like to tie their flies weighted. I have found however that the added bulk doesn't help the contour of the fly—this is particularly noticeable when you're dealing with a slim-bodied nymph. Also, weighted nymphs just don't act naturally in the water.

I prefer to weight my leader instead of my flies . . . and on the page opposite present a number of options.

> *A—the BB shot is clamped onto the bare hook, either just ahead of the fly dressing or onto the hook shank just before the bend*

> *B—the BB shot is tied in at the end of the leader and the fly slips down to it on the cast . . . used mostly for bucktails and streamers*

> *C—BB shot or wraparound strip-lead can be placed well ahead of the fly or between flies*

> *D—strip-lead attached by only a turn or two will work itself free of potential bottom tangles*

None of the weighted-leader rigs is easy to cast. One way to make things a little easier, however, is to put on two weights, each weighing half the weight you desire, instead of one. You space them out evenly along your leader, slow down your casting pace, on the upswing raise your rod tip higher than usual, angling the line high behind you . . . and on the forward thrust you aim at the treetops.

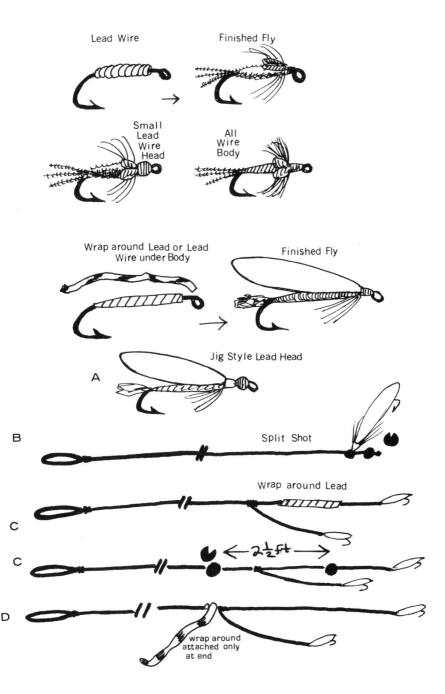

Lead Wire

Finished Fly

Small Lead Wire Head

All Wire Body

Wrap around Lead or Lead Wire under Body

Finished Fly

Jig Style Lead Head

A

B   Split Shot

Wrap around Lead

C

C   ←2½ft→

D   wrap around attached only at end

there are no anglers around to scare them. But most of the time during mid-season they remain deep, unseen, and unchallenged.

Whether you fish with wet flies or nymphs or streamers, sink those flies or you'll miss a lot of action. Tradition may make you think that the way you have to rig those flies to get them deep where the fish are will detract from the art of catching fish—but hang in there a minute. You may hook a lunker.

There are some avid dry-fly fishermen who I know who will not venture out on the stream until it's time for a hatch. "Fish the rise," they say. This is the peak time of the day and the hour of the purist. Okay. It's just fine with me if they stay out of the way until twilight.

I like to fish all the time however. And I'll work at it all day, even if there's no apparent action and I have to sink my flies way deep. I've taken some mighty fine trout on sunken flies that bump right along on the bottom, snagging once in a while.

"If you're going to fish that way why not forget flies and use bait?" you might ask.

Not a bad idea would be my retort. But I still hang onto the myth and legend of fly fishing. I am a fly fisherman first, even if I have to admit defeat in front of the live-bait fisherman.

But I'm jealous of the live-bait fisherman's success.

So I compromise, sticking to my flies . . . but sinking them as they should be sunk, right into the trout's mouth.

In the early spring, many of the biggest trout I see creeled come from the very edges of the stream—not from shallow water but from behind big rocks and boulders, from under shelves, from snags, from fallen tree trunks and quiet back eddies. They rest in such places, unless driven out by too much human traffic, and wait for bugs and worms to be washed in by the spring rains and drain-offs from the soggy banks. You don't need to cast out into the water that's over your head speeding along at twenty-miles-an-hour. Fish the shore, or near it, and you won't have to wade much at all.

There is virtually no area close to the stream's edge that you cannot reach properly with a simple rollcast. There's no need for distance or performance.

Cast your big wets and possibly a short and stocky streamer above your position and let them drift down with the current to the hot spot you've chosen below. Or drop your flies at your feet with plenty of slack line coiled in your hand. Feed the line out as the flies drift downstream. Once in a while you can give them a short and jerky manipulation, which will bring them to the surface. Quite often at this point you'll get a strike, so watch it. Or drag your flies across the water a few feet upstream and give them sudden slack so they sink again, working their way down over the same hot spot.

Repeat the process several times before moving on.

Work your way downstream carefully and slowly. You'll be surprised how many good spots you'll work that you would have never seen had you marched out into the stream and flailed away in the faster water.

There also are areas just *beyond* the stream edge that are holding places for big trout. A snag, a big rock, or a cluster of smaller rocks causing a break in the fast current. Don't think the trout are only below those rocks either. Quite often they rest upstream of the rocks. So cast your flies well ahead of the rocks, or rock, and position yourself so that the end of the drift will cause your flies to swing across the area just ahead of the rock. When the flies reach this point lower your rod tip and offer some slack line by rolling some out quickly. This will allow the flies to sink a bit. At just the point they reach the center of the water being worked, raise your rod tip sharply and you'll see your flies working their way to the surface. You'll likely get a rise. The trout has seen the fly drifting down and now suddenly it's headed toward the surface. The rise will be deliberate—no light hit here!

Another way to accomplish this timed rise in front of a rock is to wade out and take up a position well upstream of the rock and drop your flies down just below the rod tip. Feed out line as they descend dead-drift style in the current. When they're a few feet above the rock raise your rod tip and swim them toward the surface. Once they're on the surface strip in line, dragging them across the water, and then lower the rod tip and feed out line again. Repeat this process many times. Even the most stubborn trout will fall for it.

These trout are resting on the bottom. They're just lying there, not moving, not interested. Your only hope is to sink your fly right down to them and bump them on the nose. Otherwise, you may as well move on to another spot.

If the stream is really awash, as in that opening-day period, there is no immorality in sinking your flies with the aid of some split shot or a strip of wraparound lead on the leader.

If you get easily annoyed at the cumbersome way these weighted rigs cast, try spacing two of your lighter pieces of split shot equally apart on your leader. Don't just place one heavy weight on the leader. This should help avoid hairpin casts and snagged flies and tangled tackle.

With this rig you can use the same system as described earlier. Just drift the rig along and wade down with it, pausing often to lift your flies off the bottom and let them settle back into the current.

Another killing proposition—one of the oldest techniques in the books but often overlooked by experts and quite unknown to the beginner—is the downstream swing retrieve.

Trout nudging the bottom for Caddis larvae.

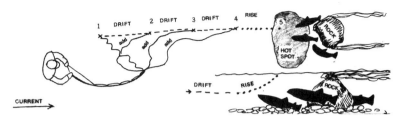

Drop that line right at your feet. There may be a trout just ahead of you. Let the line pay out from your hand and when you have about fifteen feet out, bring your rod to a right angle to the line—usually sideways rather than vertical. Keep the rod at right angles to the drifting line. Wave it from left to right, causing the line to snake in its drift and wave your flies back and forth on their way to the hot spot.

All you do is to cast straight downstream from your position, throw a mend to give your flies slack enough to sink, and when they approach the hot spot (say a midstream rock), simply let your line tighten and swing your flies across the area you're targeting on. So they don't whisk by too fast throw mends of line ahead and upstream of them to slow their course. You may have to throw that short additional line several times to slow their course and keep them down as they swing across the hot spot—so do it.

Try this technique in very deep and fast water by casting the rig well upstream from your position. This will help sink your flies deeper and you'll also be working a longer stretch of water with one cast.

What a beautiful stream edge! There's a big one in there. Work your way in gradually, approach-casting, to see if you can entice him out without having to cast into the snags. Then go for broke in the one cast that will either take him or scare him away for good.

Even under early-spring high-water conditions there are still stretches of stream that remain comparatively slow. These spots are generally just below the head of a pool or else at the lower end of a pool where the water begins to shallow out for the next run downstream.

The best way to fish this kind of water is to begin right at the edge of the stream. No need to wade yet. Just cast your flies slightly upstream of the quiet area where you'll want the action to come off and throw a mend immediately ahead and upstream of the drifters to let them sink. Keep your rod pointed not at the flies but at the top bend of the drifting line. Throw another loop of line even farther upstream and watch it absorb. By now your flies are well below, but throw still another length of line upstream—and watch that line. It's your bobber, and will tell you when a fish strikes.

With the line now drifting straight down from the angle of your mended line above, maintain that angle as the whole rig drifts downstream, holding your rod ready for the strike.

Fish this cast right to the bottom of the area and then allow the current to swing the flies across toward you. Slow the drift as described before, by mending a loop of line. When the flies are right below you, very slowly raise the rod tip, bringing them to the surface right along the stream edge. Let them drop back by lowering the rod tip and repeat, gradually coiling in line until the flies are at your feet.

Quite often a good trout will take the flies from under your rod tip!

There are two quite unorthodox tricks I use when I become impatient.

One is to cast my flies, particularly a bucktail or two bucktails on a heavy leader, right in front of the spot I want to work over. Instead of letting them drift I whisk them back and forth, making them splash on the surface. I let them pause in between rushes just to offer the trout a chance. And quite often that's just when a fish strikes.

Another trick is one I use when fishing the head of a pool in medium or low water conditions. Usually when the water warms up the trout will congregate at the heads of the pools where the

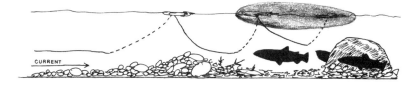

water is more aereated and cooler as it comes down from the broken rocks and fast sluices above.

These trout are stuck in a small area, especially during the bright light of day, and will stay there until twilight or later. They are hard to entice but can be teased into action if you do it right.

Take up a position well above the pool head so as not to scare them out. Falsecast a fairly long line, but when you get set to drop it down jerk your rod back smartly and drop your fly a foot or so above the hole or run you're concentrating on. Let the line go slack in the current. If he wants it he'll strike hard and mean it.

Fish the so-called waste water—stretches of stream that are rocky and boulder-strewn with few holes or runs. Quite often the trout will hold out in this kind of broken water all day long. You can awaken them quite rapidly if you drift a fly right by their nose. Again, the strike is quick and decisive and your leader had better not be too thin.

Sink that fly by whatever means you can muster and time and plan your casts to work over a specific section of stream. There's little use in just drifting your flies aimlessly. Pick a spot where you expect action to take place, a spot where for some reason—a rock, an underwater obstruction—the current momentarily lags, and

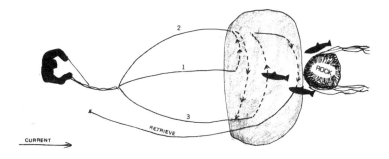

time your presentation so your flies, down deep, will rise up right in front of Mr. Trout.

All too often I see anglers working the water beautifully with nice long casts and well-timed retrieves . . . but their flies aren't deep enough, nor have they planned their presentation to come to life right at the hot spot.

There's a particular pool that lured me for years but never produced good trout until I had a revelation. . . .

Standing on the bridge that spanned the water above the pool I could see, revealed by the slanting morning light, that there were big lunkers lazily riding the currents along a shelving riffle and undercut long line of solid rock shelf. But try as I would I couldn't reach them with the proper drift from either side of the stream. If I worked from the side where the ledge was the flies wouldn't sink far enough, and besides the cast had to be a long one and I couldn't manipulate the flies as I wanted to. I had to allow them simply to drift, which didn't excite the trout at all.

Casting from the other side was just as difficult, and the distances from above and below made an approach either of those ways an impossibility.

That run became an obsession. And one morning I sat down on a rock at the footing of the bridge, assumed the pose of The Thinker . . . and a trick came to me that I thought just might do the old boys in. I reached for my leader container, tied on twenty feet, and attached two tippets about a foot apart. Without even standing up or casting I loaded the rig with three nymphs and fed the leader and flies out into the current that flowed rather fast just below the bridge. By mending line and angling the drift I was able to guide those flies right down along the ledge of the undercut shelf and when I figured they were about to the end of the section of rock I gently raised my rod tip. Hand over hand I began retrieving line. At this point I didn't have any idea where the flies were except that they must be travelling right along as I intended them to, right next to the ledge.

Then I saw the lazy S-curve of my floating line straighten out and instinctively I struck.

Ah *hah*!

I got as much of a kick out of that little experiment as I've

ever gotten from any of the complicated patterns I develop to entice the experts at club meetings.

I felt like a little kid that had just found the candy jar.

Sunken-fly fishing involves more than merely sinking your fly
and dragging it helter-skelter about the stream however.

It involves thinking. It requires a slow approach to the streamside, a hard look at the currents, a careful figuring of the angles,

and finally the devising of a strategy that will cause those flies to act the way you want them to. You may want them to dead drift. You may want them to go deep and then rise dramatically, right at the hot spot, right in front of the trout. You may want them to swing around into a particular position from which you can retrieve them upstream.

Or—if the water seems dead and nothing's doing no matter what you try—you may want them hardly to move at all. This can be worked only in very, very slow water—or a lake. The idea is simply to get those wet flies down on the bottom and let them stay there, stay there until you get bored . . . then twitch them a bit—just a little—and let them sit there as before. Repeat this super-slow action and be patient. Sometimes those fish (especially the larger ones) that are just lazily and sluggishly hanging there on the bottom with no apparent interest in anything will become fascinated by that little fly moving around so slowly in the corner of their eye.

You can only do it in slow water, and it doesn't work every time . . . but when it does you can take a fish everyone else has given up on.

And when they ask you what you caught him on of course you say: "Common sense."

Before I leave the subject of sinking your fly, a word on the Muddler Minnow.

The first time I ever saw one was when Al McClane, then the fishing editor of FIELD & STREAM, and I were fishing the water below the junction pool on the Beaverkill. The water we were working was broad, with a lot of deep runs. Ordinarily I would've fished with weighted nymphs, or a streamer or bucktail—but Al was gung ho for the Muddler, and after he had taken a smallmouth bass and two nice trout on it I waded over with my hand out.

I suppose this piece of writing would suffer if I now stated that the Muddler did not produce for me that day . . . but that is exactly what I must report.

I didn't catch a fish.

The Muddler Minnow takes handling, a fact I had to learn the hard way. Many an article will tell you that this fly is a standard old reliable, one you can depend on when all else fails. And many a fisherman who believes this just casts his Muddler out and depends on publicity to bring the hits.

But you have to activate that little devil. *And you have to sink it well down to the bottom.* The fish it imitates is not an ordinary minnow or dace. It's a little critter that hugs the stream bottom, seldom venturing far above the bottom rocks. So if you're going to fish the Muddler Minnow, get that fly *down* and make it *stay* down. Give it short twitches, with varying pauses in between, to make it look like the real thing.

Contrary to popular belief the Muddler is not the answer to all prayers.

But it will get results, if fished low and hard enough.

And the point I'm trying to make here of course is that different wets need to be fished different ways. A wet fly—or a dry or a nymph for that matter—has its own personality, not unlike a spinning lure, and to maximize its effectiveness the angler would do well to learn just how it wants to be fished, practice the technique, and employ it whenever fishing that particular fly.

Striking, Playing, and Landing

You're onto a big one! Raise that rod tip! Strip in line! Don't use the reel! Keep that line you're stripping in coiled in your hand! Watch out! He's pulling too hard! Release some line! He's heading for a snag! Drag him out of there!

. . . you want to try and get below him. Wade down while he's out there in the pool and get below him. Careful wading—don't stumble—and keep that rod tip high (it's your insurance against a sudden rush).

There he goes. Release the line. Now he's slacking off—raise your rod tip and strip in line. More line in. More. Now switch hands and reel in some of that slack. Oops, there he goes again . . . strip off line from the reel and feed it to him. . . .

Finally the rushes become less strong and the trout begins to come in close to the rod tip.

Now you hold the line in your rod hand with a little slack in case you need it. Reach for your net. Keep that rod UP. Especially now, because if he lunges suddenly and your line and leader are straight out he'll bust you up.

Submerge your net. Don't go swiping at the fish as if you were playing tennis. Put the net half under water. Lead the trout down to it. That's better. Oops—he doesn't want to give in yet. Let some of that slack loose. Drop the net and gather up the slack and reel some of it in. Pick the net up and submerge it. OK now careful, lead him into the net or let him drop downstream into it and don't move it until he's well under the hoop.

OK now raise it up.

Got him!

That was a hair-raising sequence, and if you are an expert and have taught a beginner to handle that speckled bolt of lightning, you know what I mean. . . .

Then you find out later he didn't hear a word you were yelling!

What if that trout had been four or five inches longer and he'd tried to land it in fast water?

There's very little written about this most important phase of angling. So let's get into the action and try and supply some answers.

First of all remember that for the small fish—trout, panfish and small bass—the reel is used only as a line carrier. You do all the striking, playing and landing by the manipulation of the line. If your reel has a built-in drag it's best to have set it so there's some tension in case you yank too hard and cause a backlash. If you don't have this adjustment you have to take line from the reel gently. You can palm the reel with your rod hand to control the line.

Striking a trout must be a well-timed and not-too-strong action. You're using a very light leader, especially if you're fishing a dry fly, and your tippet tests out at a pound. A one-pound fish hanging limp on the leader would probably break it, since the knot cuts down the pound test by as much as fifteen percent.

Don't be fooled by a light hit. Many trout will suck in an insect, and your fly as well—without slashing. This usually happens in quiet water or when your fly is drifting. The strike could be coming from a 6-incher or a 16-incher. This is particularly true when you're using small dry flies or small nymphs. So keep your strike light but firm enough to hook the fish.

While it is often necessary to strike to hook a fish, there are cushions available to you. The first is your hand. For ordinary small fish you are working the line from the reel, and on the strike you can control your pressure by releasing line. If you come back too hard on the rod you can ease the pressure by allowing the line to slip through your fingers on impact . . . then snub it later to control the fish's first run.

Another cushion is the rod itself. Keep the rod pointed up at all times when you're fishing. Or, if you're working the line so your flies will drift naturally and your rod is held at the horizontal, then angle your rod back at right angles to your line. In either case the rod will cushion the fish's strike and your reactive strike. Your line hand controls the line. If the fish hits and hooks himself, that part of the sequence is done for you. Don't let your line go slack, because if the fish is only lightly hooked it can escape the barb easily.

A third cushion can be created, if necessary, by placing the line under your rod hand and either feeding it out from there to

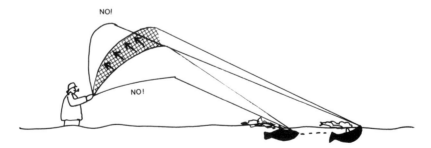

When playing a good trout you of course keep your rod tip up—but not all the way. Do your work in the one- to two-o'clock area. Don't let it get back to vertical. This is hard on your wrist, and your rod, bent now practically to the maximum (if it's a big enough fish) has nothing left to offer by way of cushioning power.

the rod, or when pulling it in with the line hand allowing it to slip under the rod hand.

The strike from a big fish may be short and heavy, so that high rod position is most important. Once a big fish starts to take off the rod must be the ultimate cushion in the battle.

One of the best ways I know to get the feel of your tackle and its potential power and safety-margin in striking and playing is a routine I use when teaching beginners.

Take your fly rod, rig it up, and attach a leader tapered down to 4X. Now attach that leader tippet to a tree or some other solid object and walk out the line for about fifty feet. Point the rod directly at the line so you can note the pulling strength of that leader, and pull until she snaps. This should help show you what happens if you don't keep that rod up (or back at right angles to your line) as a cushion.

Now retie the leader and again walk back the fifty feet. With the rod pointed up or held back at right angles on the horizontal, pull—slowly—until the leader snaps.

See? This way it takes a lot more pressure to break even a 4X tippet!

Now tie it in again and walk back. This time when you strike keep the rod high, holding the line in your left hand, and when you exert the sudden pressure of the strike allow some line to slip through your fingers.

You should feel a substantially better safety margin this time.

(The backyard exercise of rigging up and tying your tippet to a tree and pulling is useful also in giving you a feel for the different breaking points of different leaders and tippets, from O–X all the way up to the flimsiest leader-and-tippet manufactured.)

Another factor in hooking your fish is the manner in which you present your fly. On a downstream drift for example—or even a drift that has started by an across-stream cast—the slack line-angle from your rod to the leader can act as a drag. In several parts of this book we refer to using the line as the bobber. It also acts as a drag—sufficient to set the hook into the trout without your having to strike at all!

You will use rod and hand as cushions when hooking onto salmon and tarpon . . . but when the big boys begin their run your reel—not your hand—will act as cushion. Keep your hand off until it becomes necessary to strip in line. And even then it is advisable not to strip by hand, since the fish may make a sudden run and burn your fingers. Use the reel now exclusively. When you get in some slack from a relaxed run of the fish, or if he runs toward you, or if you're able to gain line by pumping the rod (raising it to gain line sharply), then lower it fast and you can reel in the slack quickly. Be careful however, since the fish can make a lunge while this is going on and you'll likely be caught off guard.

With medium-sized fish, like a big smallmouth bass or a school-size striped bass, you can gradually begin to use your line hand as well as the reel. But be careful to keep that slack line untangled.

The hardest part of the playing is in the changeover of the rod from one hand to the other. Assuming you're righthanded: you are playing the fish with the rod in your right hand and your left hand is used for stripping line off the reel or stripping line in (always taking hold of it just before the first line guide) when you can gain slack.

When it comes time to reel in, you have accumulated the slack either in coils in the line hand or in a long loop of slack that is dangling in the water or in the boat. Now you have to switch the rod to your left hand, grasping the line quickly with your right and controlling the line's outflow as the fish runs.

This switching should be practiced until you are thoroughly familiar with the sequence.

Remember, in playing your fish your aim is to gain as much line as quickly as possible, particularly in the case of bonefish and salmon, who like to run your line out unmercifully.

This is the fun part of the game and when you are thoroughly familiar with all the moves it is the delight of fishing.

Handling the jump is when most anglers will panic—and when it's a big bass or landlocked salmon bulldogging the surface there can be as many as twenty jumps before the fish begins to tire.

When you see it coming up for the jump, slack off the line from your hand as when playing from the reel and lower the rod tip. But when he makes his re-entry bring the tip back up again. Sometimes a fisherman will forget this second important move. They remember to get the rod tip down fast when the fish jumps but forget to get it just as quickly back up again when he re-enters the water. Just as you don't want your line too tight when he's in the air (he'll bust your leader or tear loose), you don't want it too slack when he re-enters (he'll throw the hook, or with a quick spurt away from you straighten out and snap that leader before you've felt a thing).

Sometimes a big fish will tear up the surface preparing to rush along the top of the water in a series of lunges. If he does this, let him—but with your rod tip *up*.

In the case of a big fish—say a 15-pound Atlantic salmon— wade ashore and follow him from the bank keeping your rod high and as much line as possible out of the water.

There are variables you'll have to contend with. A 12-inch trout in quiet water is one thing. But hook that fish below you in a fast current and your problems are doubled. You have to guide the fish away from the snags and not allow it to go too far down- stream. The farther away from you the battle rages, the bigger the fish's chance of getting away. To keep your line from snagging on brush or rocks, and to maintain better control, keep that rod *up* and fight the fish from the tip of your rod.

If possible, try and get that downstream fish up to you and as close as possible. To land it you'll have to get below it, which means you'll have to do a bit of nasty wading into the fast current with its rocks and holes. Wading downstream with the current pushing you from behind can be a tricky proposition and you may be in for a couple of slips. But try and get below the fish if you can't bring him up to you. Quite often if pressured enough your trout will abandon its downstream rush and trek upstream in a mad run for freedom. This is in your favor, as now all you have to do is wade out and below the trout and gradually work it back down to you—the current now working *for* you.

You've been working your rod from your right hand (if you're righthanded), but under normal circumstances, as your fish tires and comes closer, you'll want to do the netting with your right hand. And this as I said earlier means switching your rod from right hand to left.

Now gradually take in line. Reel in that slack so you don't get into a tangle.

When you're wading hip deep the current can twist up your

slack coils in a hurry, and if line is suddenly needed to allow the fish his last lunge it can be snapped up short in a tangle at the first rod guide.

Facing upstream, submerge your net in front of you and guide the fish down to it, either by allowing him to swim downstream head first, or, if he's still thrashing on the surface, coaxing him down backwards into the submerged hoop.

Don't raise the net until the fish is well under the hoop. Once the fish is in the net you should lower your rod tip or relax the line or the fish will swim out again.

And don't be in a hurry. Enjoy those runs and fights. In the case of bass, pike, and muskies, remember their trick of swimming in close, possibly to see what's holding them, and then in their rage taking off again just when you think they're licked.

The Atlantic salmon too will swim in close and then run for it. Don't take any big fish for granted. Play it out first.

Don't buy an elastic-cord net. Attach your net to a strap attached to your belt or jacket, and use a snap to hold the net fast to your side when it's not in use. This way it won't foul your line or hinder your casting (or catch on brambles or bushes when you're stalking your fish).

Try never to allow too much slack to develop between you and your fish. If the fish is hooked lightly, or because of a long battle the hook has worn a widening hole in the mouth flesh, even the slighest twist can cause it to tear loose. This happens often with shad and sea trout. A lightly-hooked fish will escape when there is no pressure from your rod. So contain those lunges and runs, not by holding too tight but by *not allowing a pause in the tension when the fish pauses in its runs.*

Striped bass when hooked near boulders and jetty rocks will often swim to and fro in front of you without coming in, or if the action is on the beach and there are breaking waves they will try to head outside. Keep that pressure on. Allow the fish to gain a little on you, and then by lowering your rod tip and pumping in you can gain a quick yard of line, bringing him in gradually.

Wade out into those waves and either gaff the fish or grab it by a gill. (Few surfers use nets of any kind.) Beaching the fish also is done—but the hook may tear out as the fish beats and thrashes on the sand or rocks.

Playing a fish from a boat has its problems too. For some reason they like to run under the boat in their urge to escape. If you are fishing from an outboard, raise the motor so that the prop is not available for a tangle. If the fish runs under the boat try and work your way around the bow or stern to free it up. Netting the fish from the boat is similar to netting while wading except that the conventional boat net with its long handle makes the job easier.

Many anglers prefer to hand-land their fish.

I prefer this system for all fish but blues and tarpon.

When your catch is about spent, run your open hand down the leader and take the fish by the head—if it's small enough—(but not too tightly)—or grab for the lower jaw if it's a lunker. Gently bend the lower jaw back, which will paralyze it. Now you can extricate the hook or cut the hook with wire cutters. (If you're planning to release the fish the hook will eventually work loose or rot out.)

When you release a fish handle it gently. More released trout die from having been squeezed too hard than from being too exhausted or too long out of the water. Using wet hands (for trout), place the fish gently in deep enough water, hold it upright, and let it swim away under its own power.

One danger that confronts us is the habit of going to sleep on the stream or wherever we are fishing. I don't mean literally going to sleep of course, but we do often become so enthralled with our theories—or so tired and discouraged—that we forget to be poised and ready.

I know I've been guilty of this type of sleep. Casting time after time with no results brings on a sort of lack of attention, and it is often just then that a pesky fish hits.

And our reaction is just a little late.

Or we tuck our rod under our arm and let the fly drift behind us while we fumble around for a cigarette and . . . *bang*!

We should work our way along EXPECTING a strike, expecting one on each cast, drift, and retrieve . . . expecting one even if we've been fishing all day without a nibble. . . .

Another thing to think about is the how the species being angled for fights. In the case of trouting, many of our streams contain brooks, browns, and rainbows, so you can never know which will strike. Soon after the trout hits however, the character of the fight presents itself. The brook trout will most likely bodyroll, thrust about, and seldom make a run. If the water is deep he'll head for the bottom. The brown trout will bodyroll much in the same way but is more prone to make short dashes. The rainbow will head for the surface, bust into a spectacular leap (or leaps), and when he hits the water for sure he'll take off on a run. He'll run usually in a series of short-line lunges, then go airborne again.

Each of these typical action-patterns requires astute handling of your tackle, especially in a brush-lined creek or on a snaggy stream edge or where there are lots of rocks and underwater holes for your quarry to lunge into.

The smallmouth bass taken on a river where there are some good currents, deep holes, and fast runs is quite an adversary. Hook one in the fast water just behind or below a break in the current and he'll head for a rock and try to tangle you on the bottom. If he's near a snag he'll head for it and you'd better have your rod and line under control and know just how much pressure you can put on that leader and hook.

River bass are pound for pound much more spectacular than trout, and even a one-pounder can give you quite a hassle. I've seen them snip off a bug on strike, especially when the fly was riding with slack line. They will bodyroll and hit the air shaking their heads like a bulldog tearing up a cat. They won't give up until completely spent. And that can take some minutes. Hook into a four-pounder and you'll know what I mean. *Keep that rod bent against him*!

I think the most explosive and glamorous of the smaller fish is the landlocked salmon. This little guy has all the spunk of the rainbow trout plus the guts of his big cousin, the Atlantic salmon. It is an unbelievable jumper and will rush your line out to unreal (no pun) limits.

But your real comeupance is the Atlantic salmon. This is the prime mover of all the freshwater fish that are strictly fly-rod material.

They seldom hit hard, since they take a wet fly on the dead drift or the slow swing and retrieve. But once they connect you have your hands full. A salmon of from 5 to 50 pounds can keep you busy sometimes for an hour until your wrist is aching and shuddering. About the only fish that can be more sensational than the salmon is the tarpon. Here is the fly-rodder's dream. A fish that will (if conditions are right) take a fly on the surface in a split second and then go into acrobatics that even on film look like science fiction.

All of these big fish require big tackle, reels of large capacity, lots of running line, line drags, and good running guides. And when the action hits, remember that big rod handling is quite different from fishing a little six-footer with a 7-X tippet and a size-20 dry fly.

During the last ten years saltwater fly rods have been developed that will withstand salt corrosion—and lines likewise. Saltwater flies also have been developed for all species of saltwater game fish where flies are appropriate.

The strike of a bonefish on the flats, the run of a king mackeral away from your bouncing outboard boat, a sailfish played from the afterdeck of a cruiser, the pounding of a surf-hooked striped bass or bluefish—these experiences and many others make up the catalogue of saltwater fishing thrills best experienced with fly-fishing tackle.

Night Fishing

If you want to catch a really big trout or bass, fish at night.

But be prepared: know the water you'll be wading, be able to handle your tackle blindfolded, be able to cast without seeing where your line's going, and be ready to fight a fish you can't see.

The best time of year for night fishing is late May to early June in the trout-belt states. The weather has warmed up enough so you won't freeze to death, and you'll be fishing over trout that are alert.

This is the time of the giant stone fly hatch. They crawl ashore after dark to a rocky or gravelly section of bank, there to cast their nymphal shuck. Then they take flight—and some of them come down on the water—and that's what the big night trout have been waiting for. . . .

During the earlier portions of the season these fish were more active during the daylight hours. Now they're resigned to feeding mostly at night. They don't like the combination of bright daylight and low water levels. Also, they are put down increasingly by wading fishermen. So be extra careful about your wading when you night fish. Just because *you're* less able to perceive what's around you doesn't mean the same's true of the fish. As the season has worn on they've been spooked increasingly by day, and they're as wary as ever in the darkness. Also, night wading is dangerous. Don't go about it thoughtlessly.

Never night fish alone, and always keep within hearing distance of your partner.

It's best to approach the water slowly. Since you'll be fishing with a dry fly, approach from below. When you wade, don't cause any ripples getting in. Wade out with as much care as possible, trying not to dislodge any stones or make any sudden pounding noises. Pause occasionally and listen to the water.

You have your tackle all rigged and a big fluffy dry fly on the end of the leader. You won't have to worry about pattern changes. The only time you'll need to tie on a fly is if a big trout breaks you up. Have a box of big dries handy, predoped.

Over the years I have experimented with several night-fishing fly patterns, and generally speaking, a size 8 or 10 Wulff dry fly is best. A thick all-hackle fly of the same size may get results too. I prefer a downwing dry fly tied with plenty of supportive hackle. Any of these will suffice to imitate the giant stone fly, and be close enough to any land-breds that are caught in the film. The whole idea is to have a fly that will cast reasonably well, not be too air-resistant, and that you can have a chance of seeing on the water after your eyes have become accustomed to the dark.

One strict rule is: NO LIGHTS. Not even a cigarette. Light of any kind will put those big fish down in a flash.

Night fishing demands that you not be in a hurry. It's best to stand by the water for several minutes before entering. Let your ears and eyes become accustomed to the silence of the night. Start to fish when you hear the slurp of a monster as he begins to feed.

Keep your eyes on the gravel and rocks. When you see the

stone-fly nymphs crawling out onto the bank, you'll know that shortly some of them will be flying over the water and landing on the stream. The trout will come up then and begin to feed.

If you start casting before the hatch starts, you'll likely go home fishless, so be patient.

While it is enjoyable to fish by moonlight, it is far better to fish in the dark of the moon. Naturally do not pick a pool that is anywhere near a street light or roadway where constant flashes from car lights will interfere.

Make few casts. Cast for the spot where you first hear a fish slurp in a fly. Let him feed a bit more, noting his location, and then very slowly wade to a position where you can make one cast to the water well above him and allow your fly to drift down to his position. Don't retrieve the fly after it has gone by his location. There may be other trout nearby. Also, since the stone flies hatch at the edge of the stream, there may be trout in the shallows waiting for them. I have watched big fish swim up to within a few feet of me while I stood there, stock still.

Retrieve your fly gently, and very slowly, right along the edge of the shore.

Listen to the night sounds. The water makes its own music, a tunefulness you are seldom aware of during the day. . . .

A gentle slurp . . . the sound of a tail swishing the water . . . perhaps a lunging sound, as a lunker bounds out for a fly. . . .

Despite his big size and eagerness to feed, the big trout's strike to your fly will be light under night conditions. You may feel only a slight pull at first, until he gets the message from your hook barb.

If you feel a bump, don't strike.

Wait for him to come 'round again.

Another approach to the river can be made from above, enabling you to cast just at the drop-off water below the head of a pool where the white water flattens out.

If possible, study your path during the day so you know where there are large rocks. It's quite possible you will be able to cast from the shore and avoid putting fish down by wading. Here a long cast can be made, but a better technique would be to falsecast a long line across the white water. Do not falsecast in the direction of the stream below, since you might put down a fish that is nosing the current. When your line is acting properly, aim it downstream but bring it up short so that the fly lands close to you, set to drift in the main current. Pay out the line gradually and guide it as best you can into the center drifting current. Do not retrieve, but allow the fly to swing very slowly out of the current to the side of the stream near the rocky shore. Retrieve it back to you very slowly, for along that shoreline you may get your strike.

Before you make the next cast, listen.

Are there any fish feeding toward the upper end of your pool?

Are there any splashes down further?

Don't cast again until you see or hear some action.

Some nights the pools just seem to be dead. Few flies are about, and the trout are not feeding.

Don't get discouraged. Walk down to the next pool or a section of flat glassy water. Stand at the edge of the woods or in the brush and listen. This may be the pool that'll produce. . . .

Night fishing you will find has a charm all its own.

It is strictly precision fishing and wading—calling your shots carefully and not wading any more than necessary and not casting until you hear the tell-tale slurp of a feeding trout.

Night fishing for smallmouth bass in the lower reaches of some trout streams is equally good during the stone-fly time of the year. As bass are not nearly as spooky as trout, you can relax a bit in your wading and casting care. You can even use a small fly-rod-size bass bug, skittering it a bit, or twitching it slightly as it drifts along.

Since most panfish are inactive at night, I don't spend any time on them—the bigger fish are my meat. I have taken pickerel at night, and walleyes—but not with flies. Strangely enough even Atlantic salmon do not hit at night (from my experience), nor do landlocked salmon.

So freshwater night fly-fishing is limited to trout and bass, with pike and muskies available for your spinning gear.

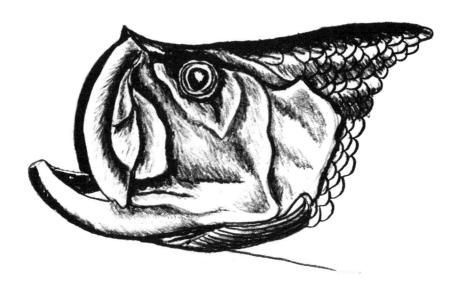

Fly Fishing for Fish Other than Trout

The most important how-to advice for salmon angling involves not fishing technique but financial technique.

To catch a salmon you have to have money. You use this money to get to the good runs, pay the camp fees, pay the license fees (and lease fees in some cases), and grease the palm of a good guide.

Then you're ready.

First salmon I caught was on a dry fly when I was fishing for brook trout in New Brunswick. It was an accident. I have taken a lot of Atlantics by accident through the years, mainly because for a long time nobody told me it was difficult.

A great deal has been written about the great sport of Atlantic salmon fishing, and I would be the last to downgrade any of it, for after all this is the king of the leapers, the epitome of freshwater fly fishing, no doubt about it.

Go forth with a fighting spirit, a nine-foot rod or better, a big single-action fly reel with lots of backing, some heavy leaders, and a collection of salmon flies. If you want to be unorthodox try some big wet trout-fly patterns, even nymphs (sizes 6 to 12).

The waters of New Brunswick, Quebec, and upper Maine have good salmon streams just waiting for you. But before you leave your city desk better have reservations made well in advance and hope for good weather.

There are plenty of reasons why you might not catch a salmon on your first trip: water too high, too low, too warm, too cold . . . barometer wrong, solunar tables wrong . . . just as you arrive your guide tells you you should've been here last week. . . .

A good friend of mine went five times to the same river in five years and never felt a nudge from MR. Salar. Then one day when I was with him he more than made up for lost time. He took a total of 25 salmon in three days, the smallest weighing in at just under ten pounds.

I can also recall a beginner who accompanied me to the famed waters of New Brunswick. He'd never caught anything bigger than a sunfish . . . but wanted to join me in the riff above the big rock that breaks the current for some of the mightiest salmon in the world. . . .

I placed him about fifty feet to my right and told him to throw a short cast toward the rock and when the fly hit the water to lower his rod tip and let the fly swing around in the current. I neglected to tell him what to do if he connected, and the ensuing battle was one I'll never forget. When he managed to get ashore with that fish he was so thrilled that he hugged it and kissed it. Needless to say he's an addict.

In one sentence, the way to hook a salmon is to take a position above a break in the current—a shelf of rocks, a bunch of small rocks, or a car-sized boulder, and cast your fly across to the left or right of the obstruction and let it swing gently in the current. That really is all there is to it. Just repeat and repeat until dark settles in. If a salmon is nearby and if he sees the fly and if he wants to rise to it, you'll connect.

Hooking the salmon is just as easy. He hooks himself. He doesn't smash at the fly like a rainbow nor does he snap at it like a brook trout. He sucks it in. No big hurry. The adult salmon does not feed in freshwater, according to the experts. He strikes, they surmise, from an early childhood remembrance of feeding on insects before migrating to the ocean.

You seldom see the salmon strike. You sometimes see them lying in the current like cordwood waiting for the truck. You might see one rise up from the bottom to look at your fly. . . .

Your fly is swinging across the current and all of a sudden it stops moving and your line tightens. When you react, you set off a bomb. With any kind of luck the hook doesn't pull out, the fish doesn't eject the fly, the leader doesn't break, your rod doesn't break, you don't get a heart attack, your guide doesn't flub the netting . . . your fish is landed.

Don't hold onto the line once the salmon has struck or you're likely to lose fingers. They really run when hooked. You should be armed with a single-action fly reel with a built-in drag that will hold back the line to a point below the breaking strength of the leader. You don't play the fish with the rod pointed anywhere but up, straight up, and held with both hands, leaving the reel alone and hoping your 100 yards of backing is enough. Standing there like a statue waiting for an admirer you wait—and wait. The strain on the rod has it bent almost double. You wait to hear the sound of splitting bamboo or the snap of your line or to feel the sudden release of pressure that tells you the fish has ejected the fly, or the hook broke, or you didn't tie the leader properly. . . .

When the salmon stops his run you come down from your rod-high position, grab the reel, and start reeling in line in order to keep as tight a line as possible on the salmon, now some fifty yards downstream of you. If your guide has been alert and helpful he has had you wade ashore and walk along the bank in order to keep up with the salmon and so conserve line. The rest of the battle you fight from the shore.

Oh yes I almost forgot. That salmon jumps. My how he jumps right into the air, straight up and your eyes bulge, your heart pumps, you wonder how long he'll stay aloft. . . .

How-to in this situation?

Lower the rod tip slightly to give him a bit of slack, but as

soon as he goes under again tighten up quickly, *very* quickly, because when he takes off on his next run, as he will do, that slack
line will evaporate in a snap.

After about ten airborne leaps you'll catch on.

Now the salmon changes his act and decides to swim upstream. Suddenly you're holding onto a slack rod and line and
you figure the fish is free. But the best is yet to come. He busts out
of the water right beside you—and all this time you've been facing
downstream and trying to gather in the slack that flows down way
below you. You have a lot of line out and you're facing downstream but your fish is now above you! Gather in that slack line,
Mister! Another jump . . . another . . . this is insanity!

Finally the two of you are in contact again and the chase re-
sumes. The salmon heads downstream, upstream, across-stream.
He jumps, thrashing the surface now. Another long run downstream with you stumbling along behind . . . and you sense the
fish is tiring.

You begin to strip in line just as you would if you were fighting a big old brown trout.

Careful. Take it easy on him. Your hook will by now have
worn a big hole in his mouth. Use that sensitive rod tip to control
him and gradually gather in your line. Ah. You're back to the
tapered section with the backing all back on the reel. Whew.

The fish circles a few times and the guide gets up from his sit-
ting position on the bank, snuffs out his cigarette, and picks up the
landing net and enters the water with the hoop under the surface.

The salmon comes by two or three times, but the guide knows
enough not to make a swipe at it.

You're fighting still, with your rod up—and he walks over near
you with the net underwater. The salmon makes a short, slow pass
near him and in one undramatic move he merely places the hoop
in front of the fish and in a mighty heft your salmon is secure. . . .

What kinds of flies to use?

There are special patterns and salmon experts stick by them
come hell or high water. Black Dose, Silver Doctor, Blue Charm,
Black and Iridescent, March Brown—oh a host of patterns, many
of them very difficult to tie and very expensive to buy. . . .

Some of us peons however have been able to develop patterns
built on insect silhouettes, or at least flies that take a form in the

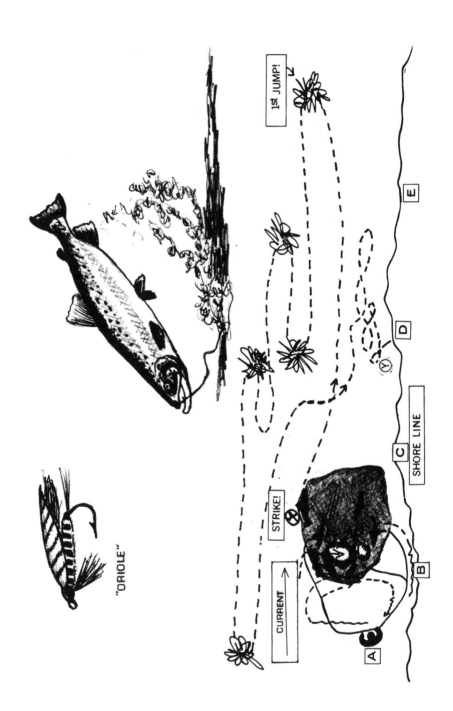

"ORIOLE"

CURRENT

1st JUMP!

STRIKE!

A

B

C   SHORE LINE

D

E

Y

Armed with my favorite Oriole pattern, take up a position at A, about 100 feet above the rock.

Wade out there quietly. When the salmon come upstream they'll pause at the rock, some holding below it in the shallower, slower water, some hugging its side, and some resting in the backwash just ahead of it.

Cast first to the outside of the rock, just ahead of the break—then behind it. Then work the inside. Let the current gently wave your fly across the hot spot. If the current is strong pay out line, a little at a time, to slow your fly's course. If you want to go deep, allow the fly to sink by adding more line to slow the drift. Don't skitter the fly. Don't make your casts too close together. You might put a fish down.

When a salmon strikes and is hooked he will generally start out with a downstream rush. As he begins to get out there beyond a hundred feet, start to give him the butt: raise your rod tip and really bend into him. When he's had enough he'll let you know with a mighty jump. Likely as not he'll head back upstream and bust out again in a leap (all that slack line!). Downstream again for a short run, up for a look at the sky, and back upstream again—right at you. He might even throw spray in your face.

You work him from the bank, from C and D and E. When at last he begins to localize his runs, at D say, you can begin thinking about the netting ceremony (Y).

water that seems to attract salmon. Many of them are combinations of sparsely dressed wet flies and nymphlike creations. But really it doesn't seem to matter much what fly you use. The fly you have on the end of your leader that attracts a salmon . . . THAT is the fly (of the moment). Tomorrow it may be something else. My father experimented with bare hooks, and you know, he took salmon on them.

Leaders should be tapered no finer than 4X and that designation is only for the expert. Generally, salmon leaders taper to 3X. Even in low and clear water a very long leader is not necessary. Expert and careful delivery is more important.

Remember, the Atlantic salmon that you will be casting to has a long history of power struggles behind him. He's lived perhaps several seasons in the ocean battling tides, currents, and sharks. He's ascended his home stream and its waterfalls and fast whitewater runs several times in his urge to spawn. When you find him just approaching a holding water behind a shelving riffle, or a cluster of big boulders, he's tired and likely won't take any interest in your offering. If you cast to running stream sections where the salmon are moving upstream, their interest in getting to where they're going is likely to preoccupy them. When they're rested and just beginning their journey, likewise.

You will likely catch your salmon just after it has rested a bit, and just before it takes off again to continue its upstream fight. This is why you plan to be on the stream from morning to night, casting over the same water, hour after hour. But again, if you're lucky you may hit a big fish on the first cast.

SALTWATER FLY FISHING

My father went into deep shock when he found out I had used his twelve-foot salmon rod and tackle in saltwater. Just off the beach near our summer camp in New Brunswick there were weirs for catching herring for the canning factories. These contraptions consist of nets, suspended some fifty feet high, to accommodate a low-tide depth of ten feet and a forty-foot high tide. When the tide comes in it brings with it herring, but also a host of other fish such as mackerel, cod, flounder, hake cod, haddock, and the really fine but unpublicized pollock, a relative of the cod and a fightin' fool that runs like a salmon.

I had taken many pollock on a handline, as a kid, but when Dad brought back that English salmon rod from one of his trips I had instant visions of catching pollock with it. And I did, casting in the confines of the weir.

After Dad had calmed down a bit we drove down to Passa-maquody Bay where the tide runs some 15 miles-an-hour. There they troll for pollock with handlines and any old tackle. We fished the full 6-hour tide with Dad's big salmon rod, and from that day on he was a confirmed saltwater fly fisherman, tackling everything up to and including white marlin.

Pollock are found north of Portland, Maine, with the main concentration in New Brunswick and Nova Scotia, where they are in company with the striped bass, another popular saltwater game fish that is found all along the Atlantic coast. The striper has become a favorite fly-fishing target for anglers from Cape Cod to Florida. You fish for them from the shore rocks, jetties, and beaches, usually at night, using bright and big flies, when they are feeding near the shore on the runs of bait. It takes a stout rod to buck the wind and cast those big flies any distance. You can also troll for stripers day or night from an outboard skiff or a larger sea skiff. Some of the best times I've had have been trolling for stripers off Cony Island and Montauk Point, Long Island.

The bluefish must be mentioned in the same breath as the striper. When the blues are running in Long Island Sound or on Long Island's South Shore, the fly rod comes out quickly and overboard the line goes. Sure you can fish for them with spinning gear, but the confirmed fly fisherman prefers to do it the hard way. No need to cast. Just drop your line overboard and wait.

If you are fishing well off shore in Jersey, you may hit into tuna. Then, Mister, you have really had it. It happened to me and I almost got pulled overboard.

All of the above fish can be taken on large, specially-tied bucktails and streamers, plus saltwater fly jigs (abominations to cast, but very effective). You'll want the biggest rod you can buy, a hundred yards of backing, a weight-forward line, and heavy leaders. Cast from shore into the tide runs, or into the passes when you're working from a boat.

The bonefish has done more for the promotion of saltwater fly fishing than any other species. Pete Perenchief introduced me to the bonefish back in the early '50's when anglers like Joe Brooks, Lee Wulff, and Joe Bates were cutting their teeth on them. Spinning tackle was becoming popular then, and most folks started bonefishing with spinning rods. But nuts as we fly fishermen are, we tried for them with small flies and lead-headed jigs. I'll never forget that first bonefish I hooked while Pete looked on. . . .

You need a hundred yards of backing and a lot of luck. I think one of the main attractions of bonefishing is the stalk. These fish are super spooky, coming in from the deeps to feed in the gin-clear shallows and tide runs. Don't even breathe when you're approaching a bonefish flat.

The Bahamas have been the mainstay of bonefishing, particularly the waters off Andros Island, though I've taken bones from as far north as Walker Cay. While you're at bonefishing, keep an eye out for ranging barracuda. They will be seen as a large, dark, almost black underwater log pointing toward you. As you wade along the flats, they will follow. Just for kicks, some time do as I did and cast a fly over one of them. You'll be in for a real tussle.

The Florida Keys are good bonefish territory too, though because of development and increased boat traffic, good bonefishing is on the decline (for the present at least). Out there on the flats the permit (great pompano) is the number-one challenge for the fly fisherman now. Again, you need a stout rod (to buck the wind) and plenty of backing. Permit are taken by slow trolling, as well as casting, and once they hit you have your hands full.

Tarpon, in my opinion, is the best fish The Lord ever produced. This monster combines the leaping and jumping ability of the Atlantic salmon, the surface thrashing capability of the muskellunge, the dogged fight of the smallmouth bass, the persnickety nature of the brown trout, and the running ability of the bonefish.

Take the small school tarpon found in the canals in Florida. You can cast for them with a light trout rod and your regulation freshwater bucktails and streamers. They'll run three to five pounds and jump like crazy. These little guys are spooky however, so cast carefully.

When it comes to the big time—those that weigh 50 pounds and up, you'll need a good guide to poll your skiff. It's almost impossible to find good tarpon of a large size without the aid of a guide.

The most popular small fish in Florida is the sea trout, related closely to the spotted weakfish of Long Island. Sea trout abound along the entire Florida coast, and so-called *'gator trout* are taken from the inland waterways and estuaries from the top of the state to the bottom. If you can make a streamer fly act like a shrimp you're in business. They'll also take popping bass bugs, fished just after daybreak on the flats. Indian River county, on the east coast, near Cape Canaveral, is a hot spot. My best from that water weighed in at 11 pounds—taken on a size 10 streamer (on a 3X leader yet!).

But you had better not leave Florida without an encounter with a snook. This is a prime fish, one of the best tasting in the world. Found in company with the sea trout and tarpon, the snook acts like a bass, a pike, and sometimes a salmon (when it comes to jumps). It's a superb fly fishing challenge and can be taken on fly-rod jigs, bucktails, streamers, and popping plugs. The time to fish for snook is in the middle of the night when the mosquitoes are out in force. Again, you'll need lots of backing, a stout rod, and a good guide to show you where the fish are and how to put your rod over them.

. . . yes, saltwater fly fishing has come a long way since I sneaked out with my dad's salmon rod and cast for pollock. We have lines now that don't disintegrate in salt water, rods made of glass and plastics that will not corrode, and reels that will last forever if you keep them well oiled and cleaned. The art of fly-tying for these saltwater gamefish has begun a new era in artificial lure styles, and many of the patterns that have come along (as promoted by the best guides) have found their way into the many books that deal with the subject.

Yes, saltwater fly fishing is an established sport, art, and recreation. But I must qualify my enthusiasm for it in the name of common sense. Yes, it is fun to fish saltwater with the fly rod. But while I am a devout fly fisherman, I must say that spinning gear handles saltwater fish much better than does fly gear, allowing for more versatility of technique and a wider variety of lures.

BASS

Smallmouth bass take the cake over trout, hands down.

One evening I was fishing just below a cluster of rocks on the lower reaches of the Esopus in the Catskills. The water rushes by there at a merry pace, breaking into froth as it goes by the biggest rocks . . . then all of a sudden the pool begins, and flat water dominates.

I had surveyed the pool for about fifteen minutes while eating a sandwich and choking down some stale coffee. I was waiting for trout action. This particular pool has harbored some mighty trout: the big rainbows that ascend the river in the spring, and the big browns that hang out there all year long. I've even seen the baiters take monster walleyed pike from there, so I just know that when I visit that water, something big is in there and something good is bound to happen.

Sure enough, it wasn't long before I saw the rise of a good fish right at the edge of the calm water. There were a few flies buzzing around, and time after time I saw the head of a fish break the surface—not in a rush or a jump, but merely as a rise, like a balloon starting to come out of the water.

I took up a position slightly below the upper section of the pool and cast out a size-10 Light Cahill, a big fly for that stream (but not for that pool).

The first cast I use as practice. Then, when all systems are go, I head for the hot spot and land one right in the center of it. My cast in this case turned over well in the air. A wavelet smacked the fly and turned it on its side just as it lit and I pulled back a trifle to right it. The familiar sight of the head of a fish came into view right behind the fly and I struck even before feeling anything on the line. Instantly the air was full of bubbles and the fish shook to the surface in a fury. I knew it was no trout. It was a bass, and I prepared for a grand tussle. That three-pounder really jumped his worth in gold and rushed about that pool as if he owned it. He was bound and determined to shake the hook, but finally he came to net—tired. After releasing him I gave the pool a few minutes to calm down and by golly another fish, about the same size, took up the same position and began surfacing. I took that one too. I hadn't felt action like that from the best of the trout I'd taken that season or any other.

I discussed the experience with Dick Folkert and he said he'd take me to his favorite stretch of the Upper Delaware and put me onto some real river bass. So we fished together on that stretch one evening and the action I experienced made me a convert to river smallmouths, particularly when taken on a fly rod.

We dined well at a local eatery and visited with some of Dick's friends at the local tackle store, and then he announced it was time to go. I thought he meant go home, as it was then about ten o'clock at night, but I soon found myself back out on the water and hard at work. . . .

Smallmouths on a dry fly at night on a broad river. What a thrill it was. I don't remember how many bass we hooked and lost that night, but we did hook and release at least ten apiece. Now you can't beat that for a summer evening's entertainment!

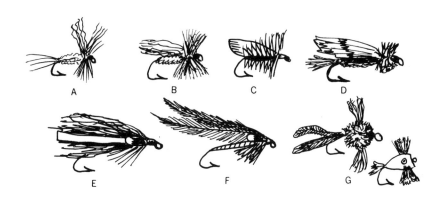

Conventional wet flies, nymphs, streamers, and bucktails—those you'd go for trout with—will suffice for most smallmouth bass fishing. But the patterns shown above are even better.

A—the conventional hairwing dry Wulff pattern.

B—same as A except the wings are tilted back over the body, cutting down on air resistance

C—a Palmer—hackled version . . . floats well in fast-running water

D—the famed Muddler Minnow: hard to stream-fish for trout but a killer on all bass types in both river and lake

E—the conventional bucktail with mylar strips for added attracting power

F—the conventional streamer: to be cast or trolled in smallmouth water

G—the bass bug: comes in many sizes and patterns and is great for popping into the holes and rock washes at night . . . cast these with a nine-and-a-half-foot stiff-action fly rod using a big reel, one you can get 50 yds. of level backing on . . . your line should be a well-balanced "bug taper": weight-forward-tapered-floating—five- to seven-foot leader tapered to 3x

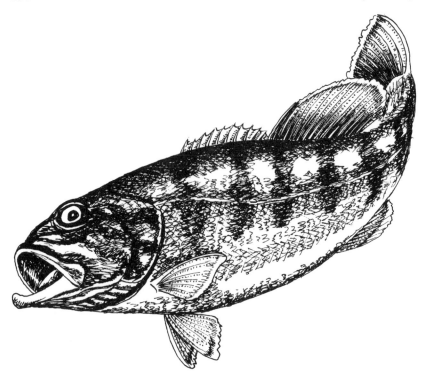

The smallmouth bass . . . not as wily as the brown trout but every bit as good a fighter—if not better!

They'll take dry flies, bass bugs, streamers . . . even the old-style wet flies—two to a leader if you like. Work the runs behind the larger rocks and the quiet water below any falls.

You don't have to be as careful of your drag as you do in trout fishing. In fact, imparting a bit of drag or skittering a bouncy dry fly over good bass water will usually work much better than the quiet approach. I like to make a good long cast straight out and if I don't get a tumble I rollcast-pickup the fly and drop it down again, right in the same place or else to the left or right. That usually does it and I'm fast to a good one.

Sure, a lot of the bass you catch on a fly rig will shake the hook, for after all, you're using a single hook, and any bass fisherman used to spinning and plugs and spoons goes armed with treble hooks . . . but the singles hold well enough most of the time, and the sport is incomparable!

PANFISH

The little sunny, bluegill, warmouth sunny, or any other of the myriad panfish species will entertain you almost any time of day. Fish for them from the boat dock. Wade the edge of the lake. Cast for them from the bank. They're always there and ready to bite.

I think the best way to teach fly fishing to a beginner is to have him (or her) learn the basic casts from a low boat dock on a pond or lake. Out there in the water are panfish that will interrupt the precedings with some delightful action.

When I am teaching beginners how to cast a dry fly I like to have the lesson take place in front of sunfish. They'll hit anything. I like to use my old roughed-up dry flies on them.

Beginners only? Heck no. I have fished for every species of freshwater fish except muskellunge and almost every species of saltwater fish . . . and you know what? The most fun I have is when I'm casting for those little guys off the dock. I also like to get into a canoe—oh it is so silent—and drift along the shoreline where I can target my casts to this and that snag or windfall. I tempt the devil and risk getting hung up with as close a cast as possible. In close is where the biggest of the little guys hang out, and too there's always the possibility of a strike from a pickerel or a good bass. . . .

So just because you've fished for the glamor fish don't overlook the panfish that abound in the lakes and creeks near home.

Take a youngster fly-fishing for panfish. Make sure he's outfitted with good tackle. You'll be delighted at his progress, and you'll have made a friend in a generation that has a lot of gaps.

Index